What Others Say About Doug Giles

"I think Doug Giles brings a sharp, humorous, bold and captivating style to ministry that strikes a chord with young people."

– Dr. R.C. Sproul

"There is NO way to describe Doug Giles adequately, so I won't even try. Suffice it to say there is NO ONE like him and I'm grateful for him!"

– Eric Metaxas

"Doug Giles, the perfect dynamite needed to ignite a fire in the belly of every man, woman and child to live like warriors."

-- Lieutenant Colonel Allen B. West

"Doug Giles speaks the truth ... he's a societal watchdog ... a funny bastard."

– Ted Nugent

"Doug Giles is a good man, and his bambinas are fearless. His girls Hannah and Regis Giles are indefatigable. I admire the Giles clan from afar."

– Dennis Miller

"Doug Giles must be some kind of a great guy if CNN wants to impugn him."

– Rush Limbaugh

Dedication

This book is dedicated to the Giles ladies:
Mary Margaret, Hannah and Regis.
Three biblical badass women that
I am very blessed to know and love.

Published by White Feather Press.
(www.whitefeatherpress.com)

ISBN 978-1-61808-199-5

Printed in the United States of America

Cover art by Doug Giles, DougGiles.art.
Cover design by David Bugnon and mobopolis.com

Biblical Badasses:
The Women

Written by
Doug Giles

Table of Contents

Introduction

Before I became a Christian, religious women used to scare the bejesus out of me.

Here's the kind of "Christian Women" I was exposed to from the time I was a wee lad up until my early twenties when I was a really lost lout.

The "Televangelist Women".

When I was little, my parents would take us on vacation to my aunt's house and they always had the PTL Club playing on the boob tube. For those who haven't heard my testimony, I never, as in ever, set foot in a church until The Trinity gangtackled me in 1983. Ergo, I didn't have a flippin' clue what Christianity was all about other than this weird crap I waswatching on Christian Television and the lame stuff I saw, from a distance, of high school Christian youth groups.

Via PTL, I learned that Christian women preferred the gaudiest, God-awful, wardrobes known to mankind. I also learned their penchants for interior design made Gianni Versace seem like a penitent Scandinavian monk.

The Christian women I saw via television ...

    1. had bouffant hairdos,

    2. ocean buoy-like fake tatas,

    3. tarantula sized eyelashes,

    4. lounged on pagodas,

    5. boasted about their air-conditioned dog houses,

6. spoke in tongues on the air,

7. had this nasal harpy cadence when they spoke,

8. and wept abnormally about ... well ... everything.

After several summers of watching that Cirque du Freak I finally understood why Dr. Chilton chose Christian TV as a form of punishment for Hannibal when the cannibal would not cooperate with Frederick's edicts. Good Lawd, folks ...that stuff'll curl straight hair.

The "Ugliness is Holiness" Lady.

On the other end of ostentatious and obnoxious spectrum of Christian women I interfaced with was a "makeup is evil and working out is worldly" obese Pentecostal gal who looked like Gary Busey in a mousy grey frazzled Rapunzel wig and a tent sized and tattered, Ketchup-stained, *Little House On The Prairie* dress.

Her lesson to *moi* was L'Oreal, Jenny Craig, shampoo, soap, and deodorant is the Devil. You could smell her before you could see her and all this shabbiness and squalor was because, according to her, God likes you better when you don't bathe or brush your teeth.

The "Everything's The Devil" Woman.

There was this one Christian lady that used to freak me and my buddy out when she would come into the gas station where we worked. As a teen, I loved rock-n-roll (and I still do) and we always had the rock station on in the background while we pumped petrol.
Every time this particular Christian woman would come in, she'd warn us about the evils of listening to "The Devil's Music". Now, mind you, it wasn't the Ozzy Osbourne only

station we were listening to. It wasn't the Black Sabbath Channel. It's wasn't the Sex Pistols 24/7 frequency. It was just good old rock-n-roll. Y'know, guys like Sammy Hagar, Bob Seger, The Eagles, Boston, Kansas, Foreigner, and The Cars, etc.

However, according to this lady, when the aforementioned and their rock colleagues cut an album and the record players' needle released the sound on that vinyl LP, demons were unleashed from the pits of hell via those vibrations into the atmosphere to possess our young and untethered sin-laden souls.

I'm not lying.

I'll never forget her warning us repeatedly about devils and records.

One night I was sitting down at work eating my dinner that consisted of a very tough chicken fried steak and some Del Monte green beans. I had a mouth full of green beans that stood agape as she flailed her arms to the "demon music", attempting to show, through gesticulations, with her arms and legs akimbo, how many demons were now inhabiting Bolton's Gas Station because Huey Lewis and The News were singing on the radio, "Stuck With You." She sounded like Bobby Boucher's mama.

My buddy and I exchanged a little unspoken eye comms which essentially said to each other, "this chick is whacked and let's end this Salem Witch Hunt, ASAP." To wit, we then told her, "Well, that's interesting, but excuse us while we go help our customers and good luck trying to perform an exorcism on our Panasonic."

The "You're Lucky You're Not Dead And In Hell" Girl.

Another Christian gal that I had the displeasure of meeting

was a graceless *señorita* that really didn't mind if I were to roast on Dante's grill for all eternity.

One Monday morning, after a weekend of partying, I was sitting in my high school psychology class trying to remember aloud what me and my posse had done during the last drug and booze filled weekend.

Yep, I was no saint and I didn't pretend to be. I took notes during *Fast Times At Ridgemont High* and then imitated what I saw in that flick in real life. I agreed with Billy Joel, "I'd rather laugh with the sinners than cry with the saints because sinners are much more fun …". In other words, I knew I was lost and I knew I wasn't heaven bound for glory should I die in this state.

So, as me and my buddies revelled in our Bacchanalian excesses, this Christian mean girl said with hate in her face, "You're lucky you're not dead and in hell."

And that was pretty much the message that I received from Christian students and teachers during my high school daze namely, "God hates me and I owe Him money."

Nary a peep was said about His great love for bad boys, His sacrificial death for my evil deeds, and His divine power to not only set me free from the penalty of sin, but His power and His desire to unleash me into His epic eternal purpose.

Nope, the message was, "I suck and I deserve hell" which, by the way, I already knew. What I didn't hear/know from this one girl in particular was, "Jesus loves Doug." When I did finally hear that from another person, I melted like a dreamsicle on a hot day in Miami because, heretofore, the only revelation that I had received from that bellicose female believer was *Hells Bells* and not John 3:16.

Now, if you think that I'm a bubble off level in regards to the strange ladies I met that were supposedly God's reps here on Planet Earth, please note that comedian Dana Carvey obviously ran into similar women which caused him to create, for SNL, the famous Church Lady character.

For the uninitiated, Church Lady was a middle-aged woman named Enid Strict who was a condescending, tightly wound, holier-than-thou host of a talk show called *Church Chat.* Church Lady would have real, notoriously sinful celebrities, and/or SNL cast mates who played these celebrities for an "interview" which Church Lady quickly turned into a grand inquisition.

Miss Strict would commence the interview with feigned praise for her guests which would then quickly segue into her condemning and judging them for their naughty public and private penchants.

Enid also had a little church dance she'd close with after she lit up her guests with her guilt and condemnation which is a flippin' riot to watch. You have to Google "Church Lady." It is so funny and yet to Dana and me … so scary and true. Carvey said he developed the Church Lady character from various women that attended his family's church when he was young. These Church ladies would keep track of people's attendance and would give you hell if you missed a service for the slightest reason.

Now, for those of you who think I'm beating up on the ladies … well … you're right. Those four examples made Christianity way unappealing to me.

To be frank, I was terrified to become a Christian because I thought God would turn me into a cardigan wearing wuss who was forced to marry a bearded Amish schoolmarm and resign my days to saying "no" to adventure.

Thankfully, when I collided with Christ, I could actually read, unlike many public school kids nowadays, and I picked up the Bible and wore it out. As in, literally. I found the scripture fascinating. Obviously, I was gobsmacked by the nature and character of God revealed in scripture, but what also had my mind reeling was the varied and epic mix of humanity, and yet God greatly used them to do some weird and wild holy stuff.

The lauded men of Holy Writ weren't wussies like a lot of Christian men are today. Oh, no, Dinky. They were warriors, wildmen, patriarchs, and kings.

And the women weren't these sexless and stuffy religious hags who yarble on about the sin of beer and Kim Kardashian's butt. They were prayer warriors, judges, prophetesses, and receivers of the promises of God who defied demons and the Devil himself. The women were, in a good sense, bold, wild, and free. Indeed, they were righteous and rowdy.

In my thirty-plus-year career as a writer, teacher, artist, and podcaster I often yap about the need for Christian men to grow a pair and act like men. I've written two bestsellers about America's and Christendom's girlie man malaise and how unchristlike this postmodern pusillanimous version of the church has become. Men should flee such effeminate and demonic garbage and run to the scripture for true liberty to be who a Holy God wants them to be versus this bastardization of what it supposedly means to be a "Christian man" according to this lame culture.
And the same goes for the ladies.

That's why this book was cobbled together for you, girls.

Don't be who yo' mama wants you to be. Or your denomination or "non-denomination". Be what God wants you to be. Also, cut the crap on the "I'm too young." Or, "I'm too old". Or "too short, fat, skinny, broke and blah,

blah, blah, blah, blah, blah."

In the next thirty thousand plus words, ladies, you're going to go on a righteous rollercoaster ride as you pour through ten epic lady's lives.

My prayer is that not only will your noggin be filled with these amazing tales of high and lows from real girls who rocked in a hard place via the power of God but that you … yes … I said, *you* ... will get off your butt, quit pursuing stupidity, start chasing down your Holy Grail and at the end of your life, you too, like the following femme fatales, will have left a massive scar on Satan's haggard backside for the glory of God. Can I get an, Amen?

Doug Giles,
Somewhere in Texas

She's Old, She's Hot, She's Barren and She Won't Stop Believing

---

By faith even Sarah herself received ability to conceive, even beyond the proper time of life, since she considered Him faithful who had promised. Therefore there was born even of one man, and him as good as dead at that, as many descendants as the stars of heaven in number, and innumerable as the sand which is by the seashore.

- Hebrews 11:11-12 (NASB)

If Abraham's wife lived in the digital era, she could easily have been one of those billionaire influencers. Probably would have had her own product line. One of those people who "had it all."

She'd be that magazine-cover, red-carpet babe all of her peers either admired or envied.

- A powerful and influential husband.
- A big estate with a thriving family business.
- On the invite list of the who's-who of society ... even royalty loved her. Literally.

And yet ... all that money, wealth, influence, and power couldn't give her the one thing she and her husband so desperately wanted: a family.

1

Today's red-carpet divas might be loudly and proudly shouting their abortions and taking a bow for offing their offspring. Nobody with any sense looks to the Hollywood horror show for how to live a full and balanced life. Why would we?

Most people don't mark time in their life by their divorces and trips to rehab like so many Hollywood train wrecks do. If anything, these cultural "influencers" should start looking to regular Joes for some life coaching.

So our girl wanted a kid to call her own, but she had given up any hope of ever having one. She is introduced to the Genesis story with one brutal sentence.

"Sarai was barren; she had no children."

- Genesis 11:30 (MSG)

God said it twice, so even a public school kid like me couldn't miss it.

Her biological clock hadn't just stopped ticking. She was *way* past that point.

For her, the springs were gone and the hands fell off. Sarah -- or Sarai as she was known at first -- had given up on that dream. But God wasn't finished with her yet.

Are your dreams hanging by a thread? Or maybe they need to be raised from the dead? Her good news is your good news, too. Here's why ...

Sarai and Abram both got a fresh start and new identities as Sarah and Abraham, after being fish-slapped with their divine destiny. Let's go to the original source and see what was going on in their lives.

Two thousand years after her lifetime, three different New Testament authors lifted Sarah up as an example of faith and right living.

Sarah was one of only two women whose name shows up in the Bible's trophy case of faithful believers, the Faith Chapter:

> *By faith, barren Sarah was able to become pregnant, old woman as she was at the time, because she believed the One who made a promise would do what he said. That's how it happened that from one man's dead and shriveled loins there are now people numbering into the millions.*
>
> - Hebrews 11:11-12 (MSG)

Like Abraham, she trusted the Lord. But that was only part of her story.

Her marriage was *also* built on trust. She gave Abraham room to lead -- and to follow the lead of the Lord -- and God remembered her for it two thousand years later.

> *What matters is not your outer appearance — the styling of your hair, the jewelry you wear, the cut of your clothes — but your inner disposition.*
>
> *Cultivate inner beauty, the gentle, gracious kind that God delights in. The holy women of old were beautiful before God that way, and were good, loyal wives to their husbands. Sarah, for instance, taking care of Abraham, would address him as "my dear husband." You'll be true daughters of Sarah if you do the same, unanxious and unintimidated.*
>
> *The same goes for you husbands: Be good husbands to your wives. Honor them, delight in them. As women they lack some of your advantages. But in the new life of God's grace, you're equals. Treat your wives, then, as equals so your prayers don't run aground.*
>
> - 1 Peter 3:3-7 (MSG)

It's a good thing she was able to trust Him, and not shrink back in fear. Because she found herself in a lot of crazy situations where hitting that panic button could have come easily.

We're talking about the big ones. Battle. Kidnappings. Famine. Pioneering and separation from everything she had ever known. Family conflict.

And then there's that story about how not one, but *two*, kings thought she was hotter than Cairo at high noon.

With only a word from the Lord to guide him, Abram called 1-800-Uhaul to "Go West Old Man." Yep. He was 75 years young when his family first watched him ride off into the sunset. And she was just ten years younger than him.

The place God took him made the Wild West look like Mayberry.

It's the kind of place where local warlords grab a few hundred buddies and go raid their neighbors, take some prisoners, or even kill a guy and take his wife as plunder.

Abram had a problem. Sarai may have been rockin' that senior's discount, but she was *still* an absolute smoke-show. Next to Sarai, even Christie Brinkley and Raquel Welch aged like Nancy Pelosi.

Waking up next to a girl like that would be killer, right? Sure. But it came with a price.

They had some rough neighbors. This wasn't the kind of place where you settle your problems in court. It was the kind of place where you grab some buddies, arm yourselves to the teeth and take what you want.

Abram was no coward. He had a fighting force of 300 men under him.

But in Egypt, he's a small fish. Someone else might be tempted to "off" the old man and walk off with his wife. So, he asked her to tell people she was his sister.

Was it a lie?

Yes. And also no. She was his wife, but she was *also* his half-sister. It's complicated.

The Pharaoh's sons were drooling over her so much that they told dad about the babe they saw.

Pharaoh wanted her for himself. Sarai was taken to Pharaoh's palace, but God personally stepped in and defended her honor with divine judgments against him before they could do the deed.

> *Then a famine came to the land. Abram went down to Egypt to live; it was a hard famine. As he drew near to Egypt, he said to his wife, Sarai, "Look. We both know that you're a beautiful woman. When the Egyptians see you they're going to say, 'Aha! That's his wife!' and kill me. But they'll let you live. Do me a favor: tell them you're my sister. Because of you, they'll welcome me and let me live."*

> *When Abram arrived in Egypt, the Egyptians took one look and saw that his wife was stunningly beautiful. Pharaoh's princes raved over her to Pharaoh. She was taken to live with Pharaoh.*

*Because of her, Abram got along very well: he accu-
mulated sheep and cattle, male and female donkeys,
men and women servants, and camels. But God hit
Pharaoh hard because of Abram's wife Sarai; every-
body in the palace got seriously sick.*

*Pharaoh called for Abram, "What's this that you've
done to me? Why didn't you tell me that she's your
wife? Why did you say, 'She's my sister' so that I'd
take her as my wife? Here's your wife back—take her
and get out!"*

*Pharaoh ordered his men to get Abram out of the
country. They sent him and his wife and everything he
owned on their way.*

- Genesis 12:10-20 (MSG)

Years later, the same thing happened again with another king
named Abimelech. (Genesis 20:1-14) In case we all missed
the point that she's a babe.

This time around, God is using the situation to set the stage
for what He's about to do in *their* lives.

*Abraham traveled from there south to the Negev and
settled down between Kadesh and Shur. While he was
camping in Gerar, Abraham said of his wife Sarah,
"She's my sister."*

*So Abimelech, king of Gerar, sent for Sarah and took
her. But God came to Abimelech in a dream that night
and told him, "You're as good as dead—that woman
you took, she's a married woman."*

*Now Abimelech had not yet slept with her, hadn't so
much as touched her. He said, "Master, would you kill
an innocent man? Didn't he tell me, 'She's my sister'?
And didn't she herself say, 'He's my brother'? I had no
idea I was doing anything wrong when I did this."*

*God said to him in the dream, "Yes, I know your in-
tentions were pure, that's why I kept you from sinning
against me; I was the one who kept you from going to
bed with her. So now give the man's wife back to him.
He's a prophet and will pray for you—pray for your
life. If you don't give her back, know that it's certain
death both for you and everyone in your family."*

*Abimelech was up first thing in the morning. He
called all his house servants together and told them
the whole story. They were shocked. Then Abimelech
called in Abraham and said, "What have you done
to us? What have I ever done to you that you would
bring on me and my kingdom this huge offense? What
you've done to me ought never to have been done."*

*Abimelech went on to Abraham, "Whatever were you
thinking of when you did this thing?"*

*Abraham said, "I just assumed that there was no fear
of God in this place and that they'd kill me to get my
wife. Besides, the truth is that she is my half sister;
she's my father's daughter but not my mother's. When
God sent me out as a wanderer from my father's home,
I told her, 'Do me a favor; wherever we go, tell people
that I'm your brother.'"*

*Then Abimelech gave Sarah back to Abraham, and
along with her sent sheep and cattle and servants,
both male and female. He said, "My land is open to
you; live wherever you wish."*

*And to Sarah he said, "I've given your brother a
thousand pieces of silver—that clears you of even
a shadow of suspicion before the eyes of the world.
You're vindicated."*

*Then Abraham prayed to God and God healed Abi-
melech, his wife and his maidservants, and they started having babies again. For God had shut down every
womb in Abimelech's household on account of Sarah,*

Abraham's wife.

- Genesis 20:1-18 (MSG)

Abraham prayed for this king so that he and all the wombs in his household were healed and made fruitful.

Why would that matter?

Because this is chapter 20.

Abraham is 99 years old. If you're doing the math, you just figured out Abimelech had it bad for a 90-year-old woman. Good Lawd, folks! Imagine thinking that great-grandma's Bridge partner is hot … that's nuts! Maybe she's born with it? Maybe it's Maybelline?

What this 90-year old woman did *not* see coming was that God was about to breathe life into dreams she'd long since given up on.

Let's flip back for a second to chapter 17.

By this point in the story, Hagar, Sarah's servant, has borne a son, Ishmael, to Abraham.

Sarah had already given Abraham permission to use her servant as a concubine so that Sarah could have a child on her behalf. (Just like we saw happen when Rachael and Leah were fighting over their husband two generations later.) That detour through the story brought Ishmael into the world and made life really complicated.

Chapter 17 was different. God had pulled Abraham aside

a couple of times before that to change his life with a promise from Heaven. This time it was intensely personal ... God changed his name *and* his wife's name.

God recalibrated Abraham's expectations about what exactly that promise meant.

For one thing, Ishmael was not the child God had promised to provide Abraham. Sarah knows because God told her so, earlier that year.

The first 14 verses are directed at Abraham. God set about changing his name from Abram to Abraham and busting open the limits of his vision to make him see much more of a future than he had ever thought possible.

Then God set about doing the same for Abraham's wife.

Then God said to Abraham, "As for Sarai your wife, you shall not call her name Sarai, but Sarah shall be her name. I will bless her, and indeed I will give you a son by her. Then I will bless her, and she shall be a mother of nations; kings of peoples will come from her." Then Abraham fell on his face and laughed, and said in his heart, "Will a child be born to a man one hundred years old? And will Sarah, who is ninety years old, bear a child?" And Abraham said to God, "Oh that Ishmael might live before You!" But God said, "No, but Sarah your wife will bear you a son, and you shall call his name Isaac; and I will establish My covenant with him for an everlasting covenant for his descendants after him. As for Ishmael, I have heard you; behold, I will bless him, and will make him fruitful and will multiply him exceedingly. He shall become the father of twelve princes, and I will make

*him a great nation. But My covenant I will establish
with Isaac, whom Sarah will bear to you at this season
next year."*

- Genesis 17:15-21 (NASB)

Sarah had believed the promise for her husband, but had been having trouble believing that a woman who's "go forth and be fruitful" days were behind her could be the means by which that promise came to life.

But now, something has changed. In chapter 20, she's seen God close some wombs while defending her honor. And she's seen Him open them again in response to prayer. Her *husband's prayer.*

That's a game changer. Now she has seen God work on her behalf. *And* she has seen God show Himself big enough to have authority over the inner-workings of a body that hadn't borne fruit.

After the verse about Abraham praying for the healing of all the lady parts in the king's household, what was the very next line in the *verbum Dei*?

*The Lord visited Sarah as he had said, and the Lord
did to Sarah as he had promised. And Sarah conceived and bore Abraham a son in his old age at the
time of which God had spoken to him. Abraham called
the name of his son who was born to him, whom Sarah
bore him, Isaac. And Abraham circumcised his son
Isaac when he was eight days old, as God had commanded him. Abraham was a hundred years old when
his son Isaac was born to him. And Sarah said, "God
has made laughter for me; everyone who hears will*

*laugh over me." And she said, "Who would have said
to Abraham that Sarah would nurse children? Yet I
have borne him a son in his old age."*

- Genesis 21:1-7 (NASB)

Sarah did some tough things.

When her husband packed up and headed West, heading to literally God-knows-where, she went with him.

When the famine came she didn't run off to stay with family until Abraham could work out his career goals. She went with him to Egypt.

Whether you like her husband's plan of pretending to be brother and sister or not, she followed the plan, trusting both Abraham and the Lord.

She believed in God's promise that Abraham would have children, even when she didn't believe He could possibly mean through her ... so she offered her servant as a surrogate mother, according to the customs and laws of the age.

And in the end, scripture tells us this about her faith.

Hebrews 11:11 says, "By faith Sarah herself received power to conceive, even when she was past the age, since she considered him faithful who had promised."

The Heroes chapter of Hebrews uses the same language about her faith in Almighty God that the Apostle Paul uses to praise Abraham's faith in Romans.

Romans 4:3 states, *"Abraham believed God, and it was credited to him as righteousness."*

It's the same gutsy, righteous belief we saw in Hebrews. Abraham believed that God could bring his son Issac back from the dead if that's what it would mean for God to keep His promise.

Ladies, how is your situation like Sarah's? What are some divinely inspired dreams you've all but given up on? How is God calling you to trust Him for your own or your family's future?

What comfortable ideas from the past might God call you to leave behind to make that happen?

If You're A Lying Whore, God'll Still Use You Greatly

*"By an act of faith, Rahab, the Jericho harlot, wel-
comed the spies and escaped the destruction that
came on those who refused to trust God."*

- Hebrews 11:31 (NASB)

Dear Church Leader: If you were going to initiate an incredible righteous endeavor, that would enlarge the impact
of The Kingdom of God exponentially and bring millions of
believers into the full inheritance of the promises of the Lord,
in a foreign land, whom would you seek to ally with, in said
foreign land, to help your non-profit move forward with great,
Holy Ghost, boldness?

Would it be a staid and solid statesman like Vice President,
Mike Pence?

What about an internationally savvy *señorita* such as Nikki
Haley?

Or, what about some bro from Hillsdale that's got an epic John Adams vibe about him, looks like Brad Pitt and shops at Jos. A Banks?

However, if yoking up with politicians ain't your thing then what about aligning your group with an excellent missionary couple who knows the language and the land you're looking to reach for Christ and they can cook some tasty Thai food?

I know. What about joining forces with a chaste, humble and young virgin teenage Christian influencer who looks like Candace Cameron?

Assuredly, all the aforementioned are great and formidable folks for such Kingdom causes, eh?

Indeed, to choose any, in the above list, for such a holy Kingdom conquest, would be a manifestation of pure prudence and Christian wisdom. Can I get a witness?

Yea, pastoral search committees would get a standing ovation from the ubiquitous Enid Strict's out there for such a sage and sanctified selection of the proper person to do The Lord's bidding in a strange land.

However, as much "sense" the aforesaid folks make to the natural mind's make-up of the type of person "God uses for great things" the CV's of the critters Christ calls and uses is a wee bit different and most of you holier-than-thou hombres wouldn't give them a second glance but God would, did and still does. Paul put it like this …

For consider your calling, brethren, that there were

not many wise according to the flesh, not many mighty, not many noble; but God has chosen the foolish things of the world to shame the wise, and God has chosen the weak things of the world to shame the things which are strong, and the base things of the world and the despised God has chosen, the things that are not, so that He may nullify the things that are, so that no man may boast before God. But by His doing you are in Christ Jesus, who became to us wisdom from God, and righteousness and sanctification, and redemption, so that, just as it is written, "Let him who boasts, boast in the Lord.

- I Corinthians 1:26-31 (NASB)

Eugene Peterson translated it this way …

Take a good look, friends, at who you were when you got called into this life. I don't see many of "the brightest and the best" among you, not many influential, not many from high-society families. Isn't it obvious that God deliberately chose men and women that the culture overlooks and exploits and abuses, chose these "nobodies" to expose the hollow pretensions of the "somebodies"? That makes it quite clear that none of you can get by with blowing your own horn before God. Everything that we have — right thinking and right living, a clean slate and a fresh start — comes from God by way of Jesus Christ. That's why we have the saying, "If you're going to blow a horn, blow a trumpet for God.

- I Corinthians 1:26-31 (MSG)

Did you get whom God chooses and why?

Huh?

No?

I'll give you a few extra seconds because reading can be a high hurdle for some nowadays.

Especially if you went to public school and double especially if what you're attempting to read is in cursive. Good Lawd! That'll make you sweat.

Okay, go back up and re-read it again *real* slowly.

Did you re-read it, Dinky? You did?

Well, good for you.

Okay, let's get busy and dissect Paul's assessment of the person whom God often chooses and why Jehovah digs shaking up the know-it-alls.

It's clear from 1st Corinthians that Christ calls the bad boy and the bad girl. The one that, according to the powers that be, be not "good enough" according to "them."

It's also crystal clear that God enjoys shaming the "wise" and the "strong." Did you catch that?

A loving God *loves* shaming "experts." As in humiliating them. Ouch, baby. Very *ouch*.

Since God loves to shame and quash the experts, He always goes a-lookin' for the man or the woman who the dillweeds think is the least likely to succeed. He said there be not many who are wise, mighty, and noble who do his bidding. But the base? Well, he uses them in abundance.

I know that some of you are thinking this refers only to a

person's salvation and not their spiritual calling, purpose, vocation or office and that somehow Christ calls the imperfect to salvation but He only promotes the perfect to places of power. To that sentiment, me and Jesus say, "Uh, no."

Matter of fact, I don't think most of Christendom's biblical protagonists would pass the fussy current evangelical muster if we held them to their stringent legalistic standards.

For instance: would any of the evangelical pastoral search committees choose King David, or Moses, or Samson, or Noah, or Abraham to be their leader? I'm sure they'd like to think they would but I seriously doubt it because these five epic dudes had more bad habits than a moth infested nunnery.

For those who have short term memory problems or who have never read the scripture, here's a succinct synopsis of the scandalous acts of the five fellows I just mentioned, of whom God chose to lead His people.

King David:
1. Married eight women. I said, eight.
2. Committed adultery.
3. Conspired to commit murder.
4. Tried to hide his adultery and murder.
5. Danced naked during a worship service.
6. Cut off the foreskins off 200 of his enemy's penises.
7. Killed a lion and a bear.

Moses:
1. Committed murder.
2. Ran from the Law.
3. Had massive anger issues
4. Was way past "his prime" when called to be Liberator

& Lawgiver.

Samson:
1. Had sex with a hooker.
2. Married a pagan *chica* like Miley Virus.
3. Had a very unconventional haircut.
4. Killed a lion and left it to rot.
5. Murdered 1000 people with the lower mandible of a dead donkey simply because they didn't hold his view of God.
6. Lit 300 foxes on fire.
7. Burned an olive grove to the ground.
8. Could not keep trade secrets.

Noah:
1. Extreme inebriation to the point of passing out naked.

Abraham:
1. Lied about being married, twice.
2. Gave his wife to other men, twice.
3. He was a coward.
4. Heard voices.
5. Pulled a knife on his son with intent to kill him because a "voice" told him to.
6. Scoffed at the promises of God.
7. Committed adultery with his housekeeper and got her knocked up.

That's just the sins of five of God's elected leaders, ladies and gents. I could literally write a big book on the blunders God's people committed before-during-and-after their call to kick butt for Him and mankind.

Indeed, the list could go on and on regarding the massive unholy incongruities of fallen men and women, both redeemed and damned, whom God utilized to shake and shape nations for His righteous purposes. Their sinful pasts and current cruddy conditions, when called, obviously wasn't that big of a deal to God because he worked with them and through them and he forgave when they were repentant.

I'm sure at this juncture some nasally jackanape is saying, "What do the last 672 words have to do with Rahab? I thought this chapter was about Rahab? Doug's a misogynist who just has to bring up patriarchs in a book that's supposed to be about women." To wit, I would say, "Hold your horses, *por favor.* I'm about to inject some Rahab into this mix."

Are you ready for some Rahab?

I am.

But first let me ask *you* this question, dear Christian reader: Would you choose a whore to be your ministry's local contact for the international expansion of God's holy work?

Please note: the scripture doesn't say Rahab used to be a hooker; it said she was currently still hooking (Joshua 2:1, Hebrews 11:31).

For those who don't know what hooking is, it's essentially bumping uglies with a whole lotta dudes and dudettes for money. In other words: Rahab was an Instagram model.

Yep, folks. Our protagonist for this chapter in my book, *Biblical Badasses: The Women* was a whore or as some would call a …

1. Slut.
2. *Demimondaine*
3. Pro
4. *Fille de joie*

5. Street walker
6. Brass nail
7. Skank
8. Tramp
9. Hustler
10. Strumpet
11. Escort
12. Harlot
13. Lady of the evening
14. Floozy
15. Hooker
16. Femme fatale
17. Jade
18. Tart
19. Vamp
20. Trollop
21. Call girl
22. Camp follower
23. Courtesan
24. Hussy
25. Lady of pleasure
26. Scarlet woman
27. Termagant
28. Vamp
29. Vixen
30. Concubine
31. Paramour
32. Bimbo
33. Broad
34. Doxy
35. Easy make
36. Hooker
37. Moll
38. Nympho
39. Piece of tail
40. Nymphomaniac
41. Painted woman

And that, my dearly beloved, is whom God chose as the point person for Joshua and the people of God's inroad for their conquest of Canaan. Google Joshua 2:1 if you think I'm full of specious doo.

Oh, by the way, don't believe the twaddle Hollywood spews about how cool it is to be a prostitute. The clowns that run Tinseltown want us po' rubes to believe that all hookers are like Julia Roberts in *Pretty Woman* and that whoring is a glamorous fun gig that entails epic parties which leads cool photographs which equates everyone on social media thinking you're livin' *la vida loca*.

From what I've researched being a whore ain't that mondo-jovial and entails a crapton of demonic heartache, degradation, abuse, pain, and soul fragmentation.

One prostitute, who hooked for twenty-five years before getting rescued by our glorious Saviour, said ...

1. She slept with five plus strangers a day.
2. That equated 1800+ weirdos a year. Remember she did this for 25yrs. Do the math.
3. Sex acts entailed vaginal and oral sex.
4. Her trysts were not relationships with nice, rich dudes, like Richard Gere's character in *Pretty Women.*
5. Nobody brought her flowers.
6. No one sang her love songs.
7. Hallmark cards expressing the Johns' appreciation of her were never sent.
8. They used her body like a toilet.
9. The clients were violent.
10. She's been shot five times and stabbed thirteen by her clients.

11. Cops couldn't care less about her plight.
12. The clients unloaded their mental illness and anger on her on a regular basis, wreaking havoc on her body and emotions.
13. And yet, she deemed herself "very lucky" because she knew some beautiful girls who were murdered while being a prostitute.

In other words folks, the sex trade is as about as soul crushing and humiliating and as vapid as a gig could get and yet, there the Triune Godhead was discussing amongst Themselves … "Hmmm. I wonder who we could use to help our boy Joshua and his two spies take Jericho as their first victory in The Promised Land. I know! Let's get a soul crushed hooker whose life has been an absolute living hell. She'll do just fine!"

Now, if you haven't gotten this yet (because I've been laying this down extremely thick) never ever think because of the horrendous internal or external garbage you've been through that such a naughty past or, possibly, current twisted proclivities automatically excludes you from service to our great God. That's a lie. That's what is called in the Latin, *stercus tauri* or what the Greeks call *skubalon*.

I'm sure goody-two shoed people, stupid Christians, and goofy family members might discount you because of your past and your current bents, but God won't. Again, when The Trinity went a lookin' for someone they could use greatly they said, "That whore over there will do just fine." Oh, and by the way, God not only used Rahab greatly but made certain that she was included in the genealogy of Jesus. Yes, fair Christian,

Jesus' great great great granny was a hooker (Matthew 1:5).

Good Lawd, folks. If that doesn't give you hope that God is not finished with you and that you're not, "too bad to be loved and used by God" I don't know what more I can do for you.

As a former drug addled, rock-n-roll Beavis, 10th degree horn dog, and an enthusiast for all of my base, lower cortex, monkey brain delights, who never wanted to be a Christian, I've been giddily grateful for the last thirty-seven years that God had other plans for me then my aim of arduously tooling down Bon Scott's "Highway to Hell."

Rahab truly exemplifies what Paul was talking about in 1 Corinthians 1:26-31:

> *"For consider your calling, brethren, that there were not many wise according to the flesh, not many mighty, not many noble; but God has chosen the foolish things of the world to shame the wise, and God has chosen the weak things of the world to shame the things which are strong, and the base things of the world and the despised God has chosen, the things that are not, so that He may nullify the things that are, so that no man may boast before God. But by His doing you are in Christ Jesus, who became to us wisdom from God, and righteousness and sanctification, and redemption, so that, just as it is written, "Let him who boasts, boast in the Lord."*

So, how was Rahab's faith manifested? Her faith was displayed by helping out Joshua's spies via lying to her king. You see, Rahab was not only a whore, but a lying whore.

Here's how her story went down (Read Joshua 2 in its entirety for full context)

Joshua sends two spies to scope out The Promise Land who, upon entering Jericho, go directly to a whore house. Sounds like a couple of ministers I know. Men of God staying at a whore's house? Too funny. I wonder what Pastor Wedge Figgus of the Glory Baptist Church would think about that? Have you ever heard that taught in childrens' church? Christians ask all the time, "WWJD?" Well, little children. In this situation He sovereignly directed His two virile young spies to stay at a call girl's condo.

The King of Jericho catches wind of this *soiree* and seeks to end their little recon mission by asking Rahab to give 'em up. Instead of doing the George Washington, "I cannot tell a lie. I did chop down the cherry tree" Rahab tells 'em a couple of whoppers.

1. She said she didn't know where they were from and she did.
2. She said she didn't know where they went and she did.
3. Then she sent the King's soldiers on a fool's errand.
4. And she hid the spies on top of her roof.

Please note: That nowhere in the scripture does the Bible condemn Rahab's lie. Matter of fact, it's entailed as a part of her act of faith. The Bible's replete with a gazillion verses condemning lying but there's no, "naughty-naughty", rebuke given to Rahab and pardon my redundancy but her lie to the king was implicitly a part of her act of faith according Hebrews 11:31.

Let's look at lying and liars a wee bit because life's a tad more complicated than what we learned at youth camps.

All deception, in various forms, is based on the idea that you are seeking to bamboozle others to believe things you know are bogus.

Here's a short list of the lies we tell ourselves and others and how we wield them. Check it out …

1. There's Bald Faced lies like when Joe Biden says he's mentally competent enough to be the most powerful leader on this planet.
2. There's the lie Christians tell every Sunday morning when people ask them, "How are you" and the believer responds, "I'm fine" when in reality they're broke, hooked on prescription meds, and a gnat's hair away from burning their Ex's house to the ground with him and his new girlfriend in it.
3. There's the lie a husband tells his wife when he's asked of her, "Do these jeans make my butt look fat?"
4. There's the lie of commission where you parlay bunkum that you know is pure balderdash.
5. In addition, there's the lie of omission where you leave out a big chunk of significant intel leading people to believe something you know is not correct but without actually stating a falsehood.
6. There's the salvation-by-works based religious lies which promise you heaven while they take you to hell.
7. There's the hilarious lie a kid tells their parents when they say they didn't eat any chocolate when they have chocolate smeared all over their face.
8. There's the lie Christian authors tell when they say their book was a *New York Time*'s #1 bestseller when it was their church, or themselves, that spent $200,000 buying boatloads of the book just to get it

on the list to prop up their fragile little ego.

9. There's the lie George Costanza advised Jerry Seinfeld to utilize with this justification, "Jerry, just remember … it's not a lie, if you believe it."

10. There's the lie I told to my 2nd grade teacher, Mrs. Jones, that I wrote and recorded, in New York City no less, The Cowsill's smash hit, *I Love The Flower Girl,* when I was seven-years-old.

11. Similarly, there's the fib that George Harrison played on his music fans when he "subconsciously" lifted the melody from the Chiffon's song, "He's So Fine" and used it for his song, "My Sweet Lord" and then claimed that he wrote it.

12. There's the lie one of God's favorite boys, David, played when he feigned madness before King Achish because he was afraid that the Philistines would recognize him (1 Samuel 21:12-15).

13. Lastly, though this list doesn't exhaust the ubiquitous ways humanity slings bullcrap, there's the deceit of undercover journalists, law enforcement officers and our military utilize to bring down shady critters, drug lords, America's enemies, terrorists, and crime syndicates. It's called a "feint". In military deception, it's an offensive action involving contact with the adversary conducted for the purpose of deceiving the adversary as to the location and/or time of the actual main offensive action. This lie can lead to the saving of lives and the destruction of our enemies, which ain't too shabby.

Rahab's lie, I believe, falls under the category of a military feint. It was a militaristic, street smart, war move. Her lie saved the spies' lives and opened up a mega door for the Kingdom of God. It's kind of like the lies told by various good European families who were hiding Jews from Hitler's jackbooted Gestapo. Oh, by the way, Rahab risked her life with that lie because, I'm a guessin', a lying traitorous whore would probably not be treated too kindly if she were caught deceiving her king.

Rahab shrewdly assisted the cause and people of God. Most Christians would have not gotten involved. They would've said, "I don't feel called to help you." Or, "don't bring that crap into my house. Or they would've said to the king, "Jesus doesn't want me to lie. The spies are hiding on the roof."

Rahab was different. She took the opportunity to help the people of God and save her family as well and that's why we honor Rahab.

> *"By faith Rahab the harlot did not perish along with those who were disobedient, after she had welcomed the spies in peace."*
>
> *- Hebrews 11:31*

> *"In the same way, was not Rahab the harlot also justified by works when she received the messengers and sent them out by another way? For just as the body without the spirit is dead, so also faith without works is dead."*
>
> *- James 2:25-26 (NASB)*

Rahab was different. She took the opportunity to help the people of God and save her family as well and that's why we honor Rahab.

Oh, crap.

I almost forgot.

What the heck is wrong with me?

I guess my Prevagen is wearing off.

Rahab also exhibited bold confident faith, the fear of God and had supernatural saving revelation. Check it out …

> *Now before they lay down, she came up to them on the roof, and said to the men, "I know that the Lord has given you the land, and that the terror of you has fallen on us, and that all the inhabitants of the land have melted away before you. For we have heard how the Lord dried up the water of the Red Sea before you when you came out of Egypt, and what you did to the two kings of the Amorites who were beyond the Jordan, to Sihon and Og, whom you utterly destroyed. When we heard it, our hearts melted and no courage remained in any man any longer because of you; for the Lord your God, He is God in heaven above and on earth beneath.*

> - Joshua 2:8-11 (NASB)

Let's unpack this, shall we?

1. "I know that the Lord has given you the land." The original children of Israel, who were promised this very same land, didn't know this. They did not believe God had given them the land. They thought they were grasshoppers before the Canaanites and they blathered and moaned, in the face of God no less, their negative confession, "We be not able" (see Numbers 13 & 14). Rahab, in contrast with those chicken dweebs said, "I know that the Lord has given

you the land."
2. "The terror of you has fallen on us, and that all the inhabitants of the land have melted away before you." Twice Rahab relays to the two spies that she's tanked up on the fear of God. And not just some kind of watered down evangelical neutered "fear of God" but fear like in terror and dread, holy crap we're all gonna die, fear of God. By the way, the fear of God is a good thing. Google it if you don't believe me.
3. "For the Lord your God, He is God in heaven above and on earth beneath." Rahab had the revelation that Israel's God is *the God.* And that my friends, is a gift from God. Flesh and blood didn't reveal that to her. That was not mere general revelation. That was a salvific unveiling to a Jericho hooker that Jehovah is the One, True God. Can you say, boom?

Finally, and I know I've covered these verses already, but I think they're worth reading again because this is how James and the writer of Hebrews wrote Rahab, the sex seller, up …

"By faith Rahab the harlot did not perish along with those who were disobedient, after she had welcomed the spies in peace."

- Hebrews 11:31 (NASB)

"In the same way, was not Rahab the harlot also justified by works when she received the messengers and sent them out by another way? For just as the body without the spirit is dead, so also faith without works is dead."

- James 2:25-26 (NASB)

So, how will history write you up, dear reader?

As a person who wallowed in your past?

Someone who felt pathetic self-pity because life can be so unfair?

Or will you rise up, like Rahab The Hooker, and get lost helping the people of God, in a cause that's way bigger than your past peccadilloes?

Indeed, will you, like tawdry Rahab, get on with your life by following a big God who's well known for greatly using weird *señoritas* just like Rahab?

When Men Become Wussies, God Raises Up A Warrior Chick to Lead

*Deborah said to Barak, "Arise! For this is the day
in which the Lord has given Sisera into your hands;
behold, the Lord has gone out before you."*

- Judges 4:14a (NASB)

Hey believers, have you ever felt like you're the lone sane voice in a world gone mad?

Like all the world is going to Hell in a hand cart and you're the only one hitting the brakes?

Good.

Then you can already relate to what was going through Deborah's mind on the day the Triune God tapped her shoulder to step up into her role in biblical history.

You see, the people of God hadn't just gone off the rails. Nope, that train was on fire and they were heading for a cliff.

Here's the kicker: they had nobody to blame but themselves.

When we left off with Rahab's story, God was making good on His promise.

- Led out of slavery? Check.
- Regional superpower defeated by God? Check.
- Brought safely through the wilderness? (Once the rebellious generation took a beating for their lack of faith?) Check.
- Given the promised land as their own? Check.

Scratch that.

The last one was only *half*-fulfilled. Why? Well, Israel made the mistake of getting fat and happy. When Joshua passed the torch and it came time for them to step up, they dropped it and let it go out.

A child could understand the job Joshua gave them. God had already done His part. He gave them the promise, and led them to the land. It was up to His people to conquer it and make it their own. To fill the land and subdue it.

Why, my little Christians, was it so important that they subdue that land and push out the people God had *commanded* them to go to war with?

Simple. They were warned that some *muy* bad things were going to happen if they got stupid and slacked off.

Joshua, who had faithfully followed Moses when everyone else panicked, and who had lead the early conquest of the promised land as the leader after Moses gave this speech in his last official appearance to Israel:

*Now it came about after many days, when the Lord
had given rest to Israel from all their enemies on every
side, and Joshua was old, advanced in years, that
Joshua called for all Israel, for their elders and their
heads and their judges and their officers, and said
to them, "I am old, advanced in years. And you have
seen all that the Lord your God has done to all these
nations because of you, for the Lord your God is He
who has been fighting for you. See, I have apportioned
to you these nations which remain as an inheritance
for your tribes, with all the nations which I have cut
off, from the Jordan even to the Great Sea toward the
setting of the sun. The Lord your God, He will thrust
them out from before you and drive them from before
you; and you will possess their land, just as the Lord
your God promised you. Be very firm, then, to keep
and do all that is written in the book of the law of
Moses, so that you may not turn aside from it to the
right hand or to the left, so that you will not associate
with these nations, these which remain among you,
or mention the name of their gods, or make anyone
swear by them, or serve them, or bow down to them.
But you are to cling to the Lord your God, as you have
done to this day. For the Lord has driven out great
and strong nations from before you; and as for you,
no man has stood before you to this day. One of your
men puts to flight a thousand, for the Lord your God
is He who fights for you, just as He promised you. So
take diligent heed to yourselves to love the Lord your
God. For if you ever go back and cling to the rest of
these nations, these which remain among you, and
intermarry with them, so that you associate with them
and they with you, know with certainty that the Lord
your God will not continue to drive these nations out
from before you; but they will be a snare and a trap to
you, and a whip on your sides and thorns in your eyes,
until you perish from off this good land which the Lord
your God has given you.*

-Joshua 23:1-13 (NASB)

Or, in the King Doug paraphrase: "The land is yours. Go get it. Don't screw this up, either. If you do, that failure will come back to bite you in the tukkus. Bigly."

You know exactly what happened next, don't you, Dinky? Because the people of God in the Old Testament aren't so different from His people today. They screwed this up. Royally.

They blew off the promise and the responsibility and decided it was so much *easier* to make room in their lives for things that were openly at war with the Almighty.

Going to war with an enemy that is leaving you alone seems like so much work. Driving them out? Tearing down pagan altars? Nah. That doesn't seem very *tolerant* on God's part. We're far more enlightened than any of that.

So little by little, they moved the goalposts on what God wanted them to do. Until they forgot the mandate entirely.

But they had excuses a-plenty.

They have iron chariots. God couldn't mean we were supposed to fight *that* battle. It's hard, you see. We might lose.

Picking a fight with someone who's not bothering me? It's easier to go along to get along. It's wisdom, mmm-kay? Discretion, too. The better part of valor and all that.

So instead of fighting the battle God told them to fight, they compromised with their culture -- just like today's church has with ours.

That first chapter of Judges names names. It gives a play-by-play of exactly who dropped that ball and what set the stage for the horrors that followed:

- Manasseh did not drive out …
- And Ephraim did not drive out …
- Zebulun did not drive out …
- Asher did not drive ou t…
- Dan straight up ran away from the fight …

It's embarrassing, really.

How did that failure to embrace and execute their divine destiny end for them and their posterity? The same way it does when we compromise. Exactly as Joshua told them it would. These nations and their pagan culture sucked the Israelites right in.

They adopted the sinful practices of their pagan neighbors. After all, what's God going to do about it? Will He even notice?

Spoiler alert. He noticed.

Now the angel of the Lord came up from Gilgal to Bochim. And he said, "I brought you up out of Egypt and led you into the land which I have sworn to your fathers; and I said, 'I will never break My covenant with you, and as for you, you shall make no covenant with the inhabitants of this land; you shall tear down their altars.' But you have not obeyed Me; what is this you have done? Therefore I also said, 'I will not drive them out before you; but they will become as thorns in your sides and their gods will be a snare to you.'"

When the angel of the Lord spoke these words to all the sons of Israel, the people lifted up their voices and wept.

-Judges 2:1-4 (NASB)

By now, you're probably wondering where Deborah is in this mess. Well, she's the one left to deal with the ACME anvil that dropped on Israel's noggin when that generation blew off their divine destiny.

Because from there on in, those same unruly neighbors they had refused to drive out were there for good. And if you ever find yourself wondering if God *really* keeps His promises, you can just turn on the news some day and watch the Middle East to see that one playing out in real time.

Just one generation after inheriting the Promised Land, with their great rescue from Egypt still part of their recent history, Israel had already abandoned *The Lord* for the Baals.

The story didn't end there, though. God *still* loved His bone-headed people enough to separate them from their dead-end gods. Even if it would mean putting them through the meat grinder to do it.

That's where Israel began the dance of misery we see playing out all through Judges.

- Israel becomes apostate.
- Israel's enemies oppress them.
- Israel cries out to God.
- God sends a leader to rescue them.
- Israel forgets God.

Lather. Rise. Repeat.

By the time Deborah enters the story, Israel has already gone through the wringer a few times. And they had it coming.

But Deborah wasn't like so many of her fickle and apostate countrymen. She has been a faithful woman of excellence.

She successfully balanced married life and her working life. The Bible calls her a "judge." Before Israel was organized into a nation, they had no kings. They were gathered as tribes, and when necessary, leaders would emerge to lead them. She's called a judge because that would have been what she's called on to do.

But she's also recognized as being gifted by God. She's a prophetess.

No, she's not the freaky *señorita* at the Tarot Card tent at the county fair. She's the real deal. Which means, she's someone God was able to trust to hear His word and faithfully tell it to someone else.

She had a husband. And we know nothing about him. Being a biblical woman doesn't mean your divine destiny has to piggyback on your husband's. Hers wasn't a "preacher's wife plays the piano" arrangement.

She had her own *distinct* God-given place in society. And she was exactly what the nation needed when trouble came to town.

But that didn't mean she had to ditch her dress and pick up a Brooks Brothers suit. The way she filled the role of judge was *explicitly* feminine. She didn't have to sing from the same song sheet as the male judges of Israel we meet in the book of Judges. She brought her own twist to it. She was called "a mother in Israel".

Because Deborah and Jael overlap, we'll be hitting the 30,000-foot view with Deborah's story.

She was a prophetess between Ramah and Bethlehem. This was a short trip to Jerusalem. In the North East, about 75 miles away, was a man named Barak, who she summoned and gave a command from the Lord. Barak lived on the borderland near the guy he would be sent to fight.

The short version was, go grab yourself 10,000 men and wipe out the army that has been making Israel live in fear. But don't worry, I can tell you before you get there that you're going to win this fight.

But Barak wouldn't budge without her coming as his security blanket. She blasted him for being so pussified, and then she shlepped the distance back to Kedesh with Barak. It was when she got there that Deborah really stepped into her destiny.

There's a hill surrounded by the plains. Deborah told Barak to marshal his forces there. The enemy got word of it and marched against his army, just like God promised would happen. But the place they chose had strategic significance.

Not only was it a hill overlooking a wide plain giving an advantage of high ground and visibility, but it was beside a seasonal river called the Kishon.

The Kishon isn't the kind of river most of us think of. It was one of those hot-climate rivers that overflows in the wet season, but is pretty much a dirt road in the dry season. That matters because they were fighting an army with 900 iron chariots.

These chariots were hell on wheels that could chew up armies and spit them out.

Deborah gave the "leader" Barak the signal for when he should join the fight. The battle, of course, was won. And just like the Pharaoh's army was wiped out by the Red Sea, Sisera's forces were beaten by the river ...

> *The torrent of Kishon swept them away, The ancient torrent, the torrent Kishon.*

> - Judges 5:21 (NASB)

The battle was victorious but ended with a wild twist we'll look at in Jael's story.

Because of Deborah's faithfulness, that very day was the day the deliverance of Israel began. It was the first domino to fall in setting Israel free from their oppressors.

They didn't just defeat this commander and his 900 iron chariots. Oh, no. This triggered a chain of events. Israel woke up from their sleep, started manning up and took down their cursed rival's Big Dawg.

> *So God subdued on that day Jabin the king of Canaan before the sons of Israel. The hand of the sons of Israel pressed heavier and heavier upon Jabin the king of Canaan, until they had destroyed Jabin the king of Canaan.*
>
> - Judges 4:23,24 (NASB)

What difference can just one person make in a world where corruption and evil seem to have the upper hand? Ask Deborah.

God didn't need her to grab a sword and assassinate the foreign leader oppressing Israel. (Although there is an epic story in chapter 3 where another judge named Ehud does exactly that.)

All she needed to do was to be faithful in the thing God called her to be good at. That changed life not just for her, but for her whole country.

She saw a bright future that nobody around her could see. She saw the leadership that even Barak couldn't see in himself and drew it out of him. She was alert to the leading and timing of God, and she acted on it.

All of Israel broke free of its bondage *because of the faithful actions of this one woman.*

Better than that, all of Israel stopped living in fear and the men stepped up and remembered how to be leaders and defenders of their people.

What does a woman like that do for an encore? She writes

a badass song that has its own chapter in the *verbum Dei*. Like Moses did.

Elijah had his challenge on Mt Carmel. Moses delivered the 10 Commandments. Deborah wrote a song.

She's a prophetess, remember. A prophet's job includes whipping moral slackers into shape, pointing them in the right direction and getting them to start moving their feet.

It's a song that would have been picked up by her culture and it's content would point them back to the path her endless-ly-backsliding nation *should* be taking.

What does an Israelite lady from the late Bronze Age sing about? A lot of things, actually.

She sings about leadership, and how life went well for the people of Israel when they followed the leaders God called. Deborah herself got top billing here, because she stepped up when the men that should have needed a good kick in the ass.

She sings about the glory of God, telling us all about His miraculous intervention against a far superior military force. Soldiers going against iron chariots in that day would be a little like lining up Custer's cavalry against modern tanks. God got personally involved in their fight just like He did in the days of old. He threw nature itself at their enemies.

She sings about the despair that Israel needed rescuing from *and* the sin that put them there. She didn't hide the bad parts. Life in Israel sucked worse than an airplane toilet, but they were bad because Israel was dumb enough to kick God to the curb. Their theme song in life was Sinatra's "My Way." That way is always a dead end. If you want a different ending to that story, you've got to return to God.

She sings the praise of Jael, and her pivotal role in the battle gets special attention, but Deborah *also* remembers the soldiers and the clans who stepped up for the fight. Check out Judges 5:13-15:

> *The people of the Lord came down to me as warriors.*
>
> *"From Ephraim those whose root is in Amalek came down,*
>
> *Following you, Benjamin, with your peoples;*
>
> *From Machir commanders came down,*
>
> *And from Zebulun those who wield the staff of office.*
>
> *"And the princes of Issachar were with Deborah;*
>
> *As was Issachar, so was Barak;*
>
> *Into the valley they rushed at his heels;*

She takes the slackers to the woodshed, calling them out by name.

> *Among the divisions of Reuben*
> *There were great resolves of heart.*
>
> *"Why did you sit among the sheepfolds,*
>
> *To hear the piping for the flocks?*
>
> *Among the divisions of Reuben*
>
> *There were great searchings of heart.*

"Gilead remained across the Jordan;

And why did Dan stay in ships?

Asher sat at the seashore,

And remained by its landings.

"Zebulun was a people who despised their lives even to death,

And Naphtali also, on the high places of the field.

- Judges 5:15b-18 (NASB)

Is that "rude?" Is that "shaming?"

Yep. It sure is.

And they *needed* some good old-fashioned shaming. Because their non-involvement was shameful. It needed to be called out. It was inaction like that that led Israel into their 'oppression problems' in the first place.

If Joshua's generation had gotten a good kick in the backside by someone like Deborah, Israel would never have left the job half-finished. They would have subdued their enemies. And Israel wouldn't have a perpetual war with neighbors who won't ever stand down.

Don't worry if the role God wants you to play isn't the lead role in the show. That doesn't mean you're not part of His production.

She was just minding her own business on the other side of the country, but God called her to give an encouraging word to someone. That encouraging word kickstarted a national revival.

You don't have to be called to some high office to do some good work or work some great deed.

In the book of Acts, we see a church deacon -- which means "waiter" -- meeting up with a stranger on a chariot and took the time to explain something he was reading in Isaiah. Little did Philip know that this one encounter would lead to the conversion of an important official and that Christian faith would sweep throughout Ethiopia.

Tabitha (or Dorcas) was remembered for her compassion for the poor, and the clothing she would make. (Acts 9:36-42) Lydia was a businesswoman who sold textiles but became the first convert in Europe. (Acts 16:14)

The point is, there are as many ways to be a faithful servant of God as there are men and women He has called.

If I Had A Hammer,
I'd Hammer in the Morning

Most blessed of women is Jael,
The wife of Heber the Kenite;
Most blessed is she of women in the tent.

- Judges 5:24 (NASB)

If you've been taking notes, my little Christian, you will see a pattern coming together here.

God is really good at -- and seems to really enjoy -- picking the people nobody in their right mind would be stupid enough to place a bet on.

Sure, Sarah was smoking hot. But some old bird in her nineties popping a kid out of that dusty old womb of hers? Not gonna happen. Except it did.

Rahab was, well, a whore. If we saw her today, she'd be first in line to head out partying with the bad boys, hanging at all the seediest dive bars and hopping on the back of the bike of the biggest, meanest guy in the place. And she was good enough to find her way into the lineage of Christ.

Deborah? She played double-duty as a religious leader

and a political leader. She was a judge over Israel long before judges ever had those black robes and crazy powdered wigs. She was a working woman that everyone looked up to.

Those women had *a testimony*. God did something amazing with them. God turned their lives around or was working mightily through them.

But what about the ordinary kid who grew up in a modern Mayberry, and whose "rebellious phase" included smoking that cigarette behind the school one night, or sneaking out past curfew to watch an R-rated movie?

What if your life has been nothing but average? Nothing really amazing happened, but you didn't go off the rails into the stupid stuff, either?

Do you have to "help God out a little" by doing some stupid crap just so you can repent of it and feel like you've got a "testimony"?

Nope.

Meet Jael. She's exactly that kind of Mayberry girl with kind of a dull life. But when God shows up with an opportunity. She picks up the tools of her trade and steps into history. Her faithfulness gave her a special recognition in scripture that is normally associated with Jesus' own mom.

But we're getting ahead of the story. Let's back up a bit.

Jael was probably a pretty ordinary girl. She lived a pretty tough life as a nomad. She was married to a Kenite, the same family group that Moses' wife Zipporah came from.

The text doesn't tell us anything about her family tree besides that. We don't know the names of her parents, or the great deeds of her brothers or children. She was just a normal girl with a normal life. She lived in a tent, not even a permanent dwelling.

Again and again you see God not only using ordinary people each in their own way, but you'll notice God is not in the habit of repeating His methods from one person or situation to another.

Moses had that famous staff. (Exodus 4:17) But he didn't give it to Joshua. No, Joshua was a military leader, and he carried a javelin. (Joshua 8:18).

God used: a left-handed assassin (Judges 3:16-23), a bro who killed 600 Philistines with an ox-goad, (Judges 3:31), a woman dropping a mill-stone on a bad guy's noggin from the top of a tower (Judges 9:53), the jawbone of a dead donkey to take out 1000 Philistines. And don't even get me started about Gideon.

Later, David refused to take Saul's armor, instead chasing Goliath down with his sling and a stone before lopping the giant's head off with his own frickin' sword, a sword that -- when David was finally all grown up -- carried him through his time in exile.

For those of you who went to public school like I did, I'm going to make this real easy to follow.

God is *not* limited by our skills, our abilities, or our circumstances. Some peeps (including Moses) tried to make a big deal about the things they *didn't* bring to the table. But God is not impressed or deterred by the things we think we can't do.

Like Jesus with the food from that little kid's lunch box, He seems to enjoy pulling off the impossible win. All He needs is a little cooperation from the people He calls to share in His adventure.

Jael's collision with destiny came along when Israel was at war. It's a helluva way to start a story, but there it is.

There was a war, because God *wanted* Israel to go to war. Unfortunately, the guy He called to the job was being a doofus and hiding behind Deborah's skirt. God had to show him who was *really* in charge here.

Getting back to the war part, yes you read that right. God *wanted* Israel to go to war. This fight has actually been a long time coming. Wayward Israel had spent long enough in the penalty box, and it was time for God to lead His people out of captivity again.

Remember that line in Acts 13 about King David having "served the purpose of God in his own generation?" Well, the generation that followed after Joshua was pretty much the opposite.

Having learned nothing from the lesson of their defeat at Ai (See Joshua 7 & 8), Israel played fast and loose with sin, intermarrying with the locals they were sent to throw out of the Promised Land, and, more to the point, they adopted their pagan customs.

They gave up on the Divine Mandate of purging the sin from their midst, of breaking down the altars and making the land a place where God alone was worshiped. They traded that for mediocre lives in a land brimming with compromise.

Notice what happened in Judges chapter 1.

They sought direction from the Lord in how they should lead the fight. They got their answer: Judah. So, the tribe of Judah grabbed the tribe of Simeon and with a "let's go" they cooperated and took their land. And that was the last time we saw the phrase "sons of Israel inquired of the Lord" for a very long time.

And it showed by their lack of results. Most tribes had incomplete victories over the land they had been given, and Dan got chased right out of the few gains they did have.

That particular screw-up would echo down through the generations.

What was God's explanation for why these bad *hombres* were supposed to stick around?

Buckle up, because I guarantee the church ladies and pacifists won't like it.

The reason was simple: God didn't want His People growing up to be pusillanimous little mama's boys. He wanted a nation of warriors and wildmen. But don't take my word for it. See the scripture itself.

Now these are the nations which the Lord left, to test Israel by them (that is, all who had not experienced any of the wars of Canaan; only in order that the generations of the sons of Israel might be taught war, those who had not experienced it formerly). These nations are: the five lords of the Philistines and all the Canaanites and the Sidonians and the Hivites who lived in Mount Lebanon, from Mount Baal-hermon as far as Lebo-hamath. They were for testing Israel, to find out if they would obey the commandments of the Lord, which He had commanded their fathers through Moses. The sons of Israel lived among the Canaanites, the Hittites, the Amorites, the Perizzites, the Hivites, and the Jebusites; and they took their daughters for themselves as wives, and gave their own daughters to their sons, and served their gods.

- Judges 3:1-6 (NASB)

That's right. The Triune Godhead does not -- I said He does *not* -- want His people to grow up to be thumb-sucking man-babies.

He wants us to be battle-tested. He wants us to come out on top. And when push comes to shove, He wants us to step up and charge into battle where the fighting is fiercest.

The next time you're lying awake at night, thinking about big ideas, let this one tie your brain in a knot:

If God wanted His people to have direct experience with battle, what does that tell us about the Problem of Evil? You know that old conundrum: if God is omnipotent, omniscient, and loves us, how do bad things happen?

Sometimes, little Christian, "embracing the suck" is a critical *part* of the Divine Plan. We don't have to understand it. We don't even have to like it. We just have to know that God is bigger than we are and knows a lot more than we ever will. Let that mess with your neat little philosophical boxes, why don't you?

Unfortunately, not everyone gets the memo that God wants His men to, you know, *act like one.*

Just like today, back then some of the "leaders" weren't keen on that whole stepping up thing. One bro named Barak, for instance, would rather "lead from behind" and let the Prophetess Deborah stand as the scapegoat if the battle didn't work out.

Huh. Some guy with a name like that leading from behind. That's weird. Sounds strangely familiar.

Anywho, this Barak is the same guy that Deborah the prophetess texted with a call to battle. You know, "You've got a date with destiny, don't you Barak? Are you going to show up or not?"

When Deborah called Barak to lead the fight, he wasn't afraid of the fight itself. He fought and fought well. He was afraid of the *leadership* part. What we *do* know is that he was *supposed* to have taken this word from Deborah and run with it. He could have been a national hero, beating a superior force with a brilliant strategy and a divine intervention to boot. But Barak refused to do it God's way.

She was a prophetess and everyone knew it. This was

received as a direct mandate from Heaven where even the success itself was promised -- but Barak ducked and weaved when it came time to take leadership.

A few pages later, in the very next story after Deborah, Jael, and Barak was this guy named Gideon. He was a different sort of cat. His problem wasn't one of refusing to step up into leadership. He just wanted to make sure he understood the message. It messed with everything he thought he knew, and he had to unlearn some things about himself in order to step into his calling.

Sure, Gideon knew that God loved Israel once upon a time, back in the day, but what about now? Things haven't exactly been cool between YHWH and His people for a really long time. And what about the way Israel keeps getting stomped like a narc at a biker rally? It's tough to reconcile that to the stories we hear about Moses and Egypt or of Joshua and Jericho. If you do still like us, God, why is all this still happening?

When Gideon pushes back against God it isn't coming from rebellion. He's like Mulder in X-files, His question is, "I want to believe." Just like that guy in the gospels "Help thou my unbelief."

When Barak refused to take up the leadership role, it wasn't mere questioning. It was outright refusal. Deborah had an answer for him, and he wouldn't like it.

Then Barak said to her, "If you will go with me, then I will go; but if you will not go with me, I will not go." She said, "I will surely go with you; nevertheless, the

*honor shall not be yours on the journey that you are
about to take, for the Lord will sell Sisera into the
hands of a woman." Then Deborah arose and went
with Barak to Kedesh. Barak called Zebulun and
Naphtali together to Kedesh, and ten thousand men
went up with him; Deborah also went up with him.*

-Judges 4:8-10 (NASB)

Barak and his army did exactly what God said they would.

God brought the enemy to them, to fight on their turf. Notice how God was able to arrange that? You'd think He was God or something ...

Then the rains came up and took away Sisera's advantage of the iron chariots. Israel routed the army, but their general got away, only to meet up with a seemingly ordinary woman in an ordinary tent. Notice again how God keeps making these dates with destiny happen all over the place! Sisera didn't go looking for it. Jael never woke up expecting this situation to fall in her lap. But it *still* fulfilled Deborah's promise to Barak that the Lord would sell Sisera into the hand of a woman. Huh. Imagine that. Almost Providential.

Does this ordinary woman pick up a spear and challenge Barak to a fight? Of course not. She wouldn't have stood a chance. No, like so many other stories before and after her, she used what she already had in her hand.

Here's how the Bible tells it:

Deborah said to Barak, "Arise! For this is the day

in which the Lord has given Sisera into your hands; behold, the Lord has gone out before you." So Barak went down from Mount Tabor with ten thousand men following him. The Lord routed Sisera and all his chariots and all his army with the edge of the sword before Barak; and Sisera alighted from his chariot and fled away on foot. But Barak pursued the chariots and the army as far as Harosheth-hagoyim, and all the army of Sisera fell by the edge of the sword; not even one was left.

Now Sisera fled away on foot to the tent of Jael, the wife of Heber the Kenite, for there was peace between Jabin the king of Hazor and the house of Heber the Kenite. Jael went out to meet Sisera, and said to him, "Turn aside, my master, turn aside to me! Do not be afraid." And he turned aside to her into the tent, and she covered him with a rug. He said to her, "Please give me a little water to drink, for I am thirsty." So she opened a bottle of milk and gave him a drink; then she covered him. He said to her, "Stand in the doorway of the tent, and it shall be if anyone comes and inquires of you, and says, 'Is there anyone here?' that you shall say, 'No.'" But Jael, Heber's wife, took a tent peg and seized a hammer in her hand, and went secretly to him and drove the peg into his temple, and it went through into the ground; for he was sound asleep and exhausted. So he died. And behold, as Barak pursued Sisera, Jael came out to meet him and said to him, "Come, and I will show you the man whom you are seeking." And he entered with her, and behold Sisera was lying dead with the tent peg in his temple.

So God subdued on that day Jabin the king of Canaan before the sons of Israel. The hand of the sons of Israel pressed heavier and heavier upon Jabin the king of Canaan, until they had destroyed Jabin the king of Canaan.

- Judges 4:14-24 (NASB)

So what went down in this meeting between Jael and the commander of the enemy's forces? Four things:

- She invited Sisera into her home.
- She showed him great hospitality.
- She interrupted his REM sleep by driving a tent peg through his brainpan.
- She personally announced the death of Sisera to Barak.

The dramatic victory God granted to His people over the enemy that had oppressed them came through the most ordinary tools of a tent-dwelling housewife.

She invited him in. It was an offer Sisera could hardly refuse. He'd been on the run for who knows how long. He was tired, thirsty, and hungry, and needed somewhere safe to hide out until he caught his breath. He figured he was coming to the family home of a tribe that was at peace with him, so receiving her hospitality was the most natural thing he could do. She threw a rug over him as a blanket and to conceal him from discovery. This looked a lot like what Rahab did for those spies in Jericho all those generations before.

When he was thirsty and asked for water, she offered milk. This is generous hospitality, going over and above the request of that enemy commander. He asked her to keep watch, and hide him from the Israelite army which was trying to hunt him down like a dog.

And then, while he was out like a light, this tent-dwelling *señorita* took a tool she had used countless times before. One she knew how to handle -- one she could strike with precision. A tent peg and a mallet.

That act of courage earned her a special place in Jewish history, a special place in Deborah's song.

For one thing, her act of courage placed her alongside a contemporary who had personally killed 600 Philistines with an old-school cattle prod. That's some *killer* high praise.

> *"In the days of Shamgar the son of Anath,*
> *In the days of Jael, the highways were deserted,*
> *And travelers went by roundabout ways.*
> - Judges 5:6 (NASB)

Sure, Barak got some credit for fighting in his battle, and was mentioned by name among the heroes of our faith later on in Hebrews chapter 11. But the *best* praise was saved for an ordinary housewife who -- with nothing more glamorous than a jug of milk, a rug, a mallet and a tent peg -- became the singular instrument God used to save His people from bondage.

Here's her appearance in Deborah's song:

> *Most blessed of women is Jael,*
> *The wife of Heber the Kenite;*
> *Most blessed is she of women in the tent.*
> *"He asked for water and she gave him milk;*
> *In a magnificent bowl she brought him curds.*
> *"She reached out her hand for the tent peg,*
> *And her right hand for the workmen's hammer.*
> *Then she struck Sisera, she smashed his head;*
> *And she shattered and pierced his temple.*

"Between her feet he bowed, he fell, he lay;
Between her feet he bowed, he fell;
Where he bowed, there he fell dead.

- Judges 5:24-27 (NASB)

But didn't Jael *deceive* Sisera? Wasn't it *murder* to kill a man in his sleep like that? That's one of the Thou Shalt Nots, and a pretty important one.

Sisera was the commander of an army running away from the battle. He was leaving any surviving troops on the battle-field. He asked this stranger to lie for him so that he wouldn't be discovered in her tent. He would hardly be in a position to complain about deception.

But there's more. Have a gander at what Deborah sang just before praising Jael.

"Curse Meroz, says the angel of the Lord,
curse bitterly its inhabitants,because they did not
come to the help of the Lord, to the help of the Lord
against the mighty.

- Judges 5:23 (NASB)

Ouch, baby. *Very ouch.* God Himself was keeping score with who showed up to this fight and who didn't. Maybe that had something to do with why Jael hammered that point home.

Did you catch that honor Deborah, the Judge of Israel and Prophetess gave to little ol' Jael? "Most blessed of women be Jael."

Does that phrase ring any bells for you?

It should.

We saw that phase again about a thousand years later when another very ordinary young woman turned out to have a very extraordinary life. That other young woman was told by an angel that she was going to have a baby, and she should call His name Jesus.

God's ability to use you in His plan has nothing to do with what skills you bring to the table. In fact, He loves setting up impossible situations, and then surprising us all with His solution.

God used a fisherman to build His church, and a Pharisee to bring the gospel to the Gentiles. He used a Roman instrument of death and torture to conquer death and save us from our sins.

Whatever gifts and talents you think you have or don't have, He really *can* use you. Not because *you* are so awesome, and you probably are ... but because *He* is so awesome.

From Gathering Scraps,
To Striking the Motherload

*But Ruth said, "Do not urge me to leave you or turn
back from following you; for where you go, I will go,
and where you lodge, I will lodge. Your people shall
be my people, and your God, my God. Where you die,
I will die, and there I will be buried. Thus may the
Lord do to me, and worse, if anything but death parts
you and me."*

- Ruth 1:16-17 (NASB)

I don't know if you've noticed yet, but if you take a gander
through scripture, God often chooses the most unlikely
people to achieve His plans and purposes.

I know I keep harping on it, but that's because sometimes
it takes some repetition to get Christians to understand that the
people that God used weren't chosen because of their special
gifts and talents. Here's another reminder.

The man that God chose to make a covenant with, Abraham, was a coward and a serial liar, and hooked up with his maid when he was in his 80s to hurry along God's promise. That didn't work out so well. Abraham is not alone in God's Losers-Turned-Winners Hall of Fame -- God used a bunch of unlikely people throughout the Old and New Testaments to fulfill His plans on the Earth. Some of those notable folks include:

- Moses, who was a stuttering murderer on the lam.
- Rahab, a hooker from Jericho.
- King David whose seven wives weren't enough to satisfy his lust, so he had an affair with Bathsheba, and had her husband killed to hide his adultery.
- Peter, a hot-tempered, dunderheaded fishermen whose motto up until the Resurrection seemed to be "Ready, Fire, Aim!" almost every time he opened his mouth.

Ruth is a little different. She wasn't exactly a screw-up the way these others were. Her mother-in-law, Naomi, well, that's *another* story. Good Lawd! *She* was a hot mess. You can't get to know who Ruth was as a woman without digging into her mother-in-law's baggage.

Naomi was down on her luck and when I say down on her luck, I mean it was so bad that she thought that she had been cursed by God. (Ruth 1:13) She sank into a depression so dark that it makes a black-lipsticked 15-year old on haloperidol listening to Billie Eilish on a loop while fawning over *Joker* merch look positively ebullient.

It's no wonder that Naomi was down in the dumps. Naomi

and her family kept doing the things that God said not to do. Let's look at the last verse at the end of the book of Judges -- it says, *"In those days there was no king in Israel; everyone did what was right in his own eyes."* - Judges 21:25 (NASB)

The very next book is Ruth which begins:

Now it came about in the days when the judges governed, that there was a famine in the land. And a certain man of Bethlehem in Judah went to sojourn in the land of Moab with his wife and his two sons. The name of the man was Elimelech, and the name of his wife, Naomi; and the names of his two sons were Mahlon and Chilion, Ephrathites of Bethlehem in Judah. Now they entered the land of Moab and remained there."

- Ruth 1:1,2 (NASB)

Didn't God say that He would bless the land and make the harvests plentiful if Israel obeyed His Commandments? Why yes, Dinky. Yes, He did. You get a gold star.

In Leviticus 26.3-6, God said:

Walk in my statues and observe my commandments and do them, I will bring rains in their season, and the land shall yield its increase and the trees of the field shall yield their fruit. Your threshing shall last to the time of the grape harvest and the grape harvest shall last to the time for sowing. And you shall eat your bread to the full and dwell in your land securely.

God had promised Israel bumper crops year after year, season after season if they followed Him. So, where did the famine come from? The people of Israel doing what was right in their own eyes, *ergo* the land was not going to bring forth its increase.

Naomi's husband, Elimelech decided to take his family and head on over to Moab and try to not starve there. It was an interesting strategy since God had commanded His people to be separate from the pagan nations around Israel … which included … you guessed it, Moab.

So, how'd that plan work out for them? Eh, not so great. What was the first thing that that scripture says happened after they parked their pickup in Moab?

Elimelech died.

Yep, they arrived in Moab, the patriarch drops dead. Now what?

Well, fortunately, Naomi has two sons to take care of her. Mahlon and Chilion were young bucks, and, as options were limited, married a couple of the local girls, Ruth and Orpah. After all, when in Moab, do as the Moabites do.

Except, this was a strict no-no in Israel, the Moabites were the enemies of God's people and God made it pretty clear what he thought of them. Deuteronomy 23:3 says, *"No Ammonite or Moabite shall enter the assembly of the Lord; none of their* **descendants**, *even to the tenth generation, shall ever enter the assembly of the Lord."*

After 10 years in Moab, both Mahlon and Chilion died and the kicker was that both of them were childless. Can you imagine how Naomi felt at this point? Well, we know what she thought because scripture tells us. She believed that her family had been cursed by God Almighty — she actually refers to God as El Shaddai here — and all that she had left were her two (likely barren) Moabite daughters-in-law that God had *also* cursed and she was now responsible for. In just five verses, Naomi has lost everything and was burdened with the care of two young widows.

Naomi heard that the famine in Judah was over and decided to go back to her homeland where she knew that at the very least, she could rely on the charity of gleaning the fields that was established in the law for the provision of widows. (Deuteronomy 24:19)

Ruth and Orpah set off with her. But while on the journey, it occurred to Naomi that she was dooming these young Moabite women to the same pathetic future that she was about to have. She was also taking them out of everything that they've ever known into a new land where they were foreigners.

Naomi didn't have any more sons to marry them off to, and they couldn't wait even if she could still have kids. Naomi realized that she had to let them go back and try to make a new life with a new husband. She sent them back home (Ruth 1:8-9) At first, both women refused to leave her, but after she says that she has the hand of the Almighty against her (Ruth 1:13) Orpah kisses her and turns back to Moab. Ruth, on the other hand, clings to Naomi and refuses to leave.

Here come the couple of verses that were printed on just about every Evangelical wedding program in the 1980s. It was almost as common as big hair, blue eyeshadow, and ugly, hot pink satin bridesmaid gowns. Ruth tells Naomi …

> *Do not urge me to leave you or turn back from follow-ing you; for where you go, I will go, and where you lodge, I will lodge. Your people shall be my people, and your God, my God. Where you die, I will die, and there I will be buried. Thus may the Lord do to me, and worse, if anything but death parts you and me.*
>
> - Ruth 1:16-17 (NASB)

Now, *that* is a pretty incredible statement! Ruth makes a commitment to Naomi that she's never going to abandon her. Not only that, she's forsaking *her own people* and calling her-self one of the Israelites.

Ruth even says that Naomi's God will be *her* God.

What did she know about that God? Well, at this point, ac-cording to Naomi, that was the God had put His hand *against* Naomi and she was doomed to a life of poverty relying on what grain she could gather in the fields that was leftover after the harvest. She was literally going to live on crumbs, and Ruth said she'd join her until they both died. Ruth was follow-ing God, but not for what she could get out of it.

That is some kind of faith! You know what that reminds me of? Another woman in the New Testament who said that she would settle for crumbs that fell from the Master's table — the Syrophoenician woman that came to Jesus for the healing of her daughter. Jesus called her a dog and then said her faith was great. Seriously. Look it up. (Matthew 15:21-28)

Ruth and Naomi were willing to live on crumbs in Israel rather than die in Moab apart from God's people. Kinda similar to the situation of the Prodigal Son, eh? (Luke 15:11-32)

When Ruth signed on to follow Jehovah, she wasn't promised her "best life now" filled with private jets, hobnobbing with Hollywood stars, and closets full of Gucci and Versace — she was knowingly choosing a life filled with misery and hardship and no promise that she would even have food to eat.

The last verse of Ruth 1 shows the first glimmer of hope for Naomi and Ruth — they had arrived in Bethlehem at the beginning of the barley harvest. When Naomi entered her hometown of Bethlehem, she wasn't feeling so hopeful — she told everyone to call her Bitter because *"God has dealt very bitterly with me."* (Ruth 1:19-21) Notice that Ruth didn't share in Naomi's drama, nor did she contradict her mother-in-law. She stayed at her side and was an absolute rock for a broken woman.

It's in Ruth 2 that we start to get a real picture of who Ruth was beyond her unfailing loyalty — the first chapter was all about Naomi and her family, and that's vital to understand Ruth's story, but the next three chapters of the book are all about Ruth.

So, what do we learn about the intrepid Moabitess? Quite a lot, actually.

1. Ruth was a go-getter. She went out and did the thing

that needed doing. Remember that whole grabbing the scraps of grain left after the harvesting? Ruth did. She went to Naomi and said, *"Please let me go to the field and glean among the ears of grain after one in whose sight I may find favor."* (Ruth 2:2) She didn't wait for Naomi to ask her to do it — she took the initiative.

2. Ruth respects authority. She not only asked Naomi if she can go and glean in the fields, she made sure that it was copacetic with the peeps harvesting the grain. She was a stranger, after all — they didn't know her or her family or if she was a serial killer. She was also a childless, Moabite widow who was hanging with that "cursed" Naomi.

3. Ruth was a hard worker as in, diligent, as in, started gleaning from sun-up and through the heat of the day with just a brief rest. (Ruth 2:3-7) She didn't stop if she broke a nail, didn't take a latte break, take a minute to scroll through Instagram, or complain that the work was hard. She just did what needed to be done.

Doesn't that just sound like all of the Christians filling the pews these days? No? Huh. That's weird. I can't imagine why that would be the case, can you?

Ruth is exhibiting here some of those character traits of a wife that are praised in Proverbs 31, and that gets her noticed.

It's at this point that Ruth's love interest comes in. You see, Naomi, in the depths of her despair, while lamenting that she didn't have any more sons for Ruth and Orpah to marry, forgot that the Hebrew custom of a "kinsman redeemer" didn't need to be the *brother* of the deceased, just a close relative.

For those of you scratchin' your noggins about what the heck a "kinsman redeemer" is, it's a close relative who would marry a widow and continue on the line of the relative that had died. It would ensure that the property and lineage would continue. Spoiler alert: Elimelech's relative, Boaz, would fulfill that role for Mahlon by marrying Ruth.

Boaz was from the same clan as Elimelech, and he was one of those rich bros — he owned the fields that Ruth was gleaning from. Boaz was a righteous dude, and I don't mean that in the Pauly Shore way — I mean that Boaz was a man who was right with God. We can see that in the way that he greets his field hands, (Ruth 2:4) and how he speaks to Ruth. When she asks why he would take notice of her, Boaz says:

> *"All that you have done for your mother-in-law after the death of your husband has been fully reported to me, and how you left your father and your mother and the land of your birth, and came to a people that you did not previously know. May the Lord reward your work, and your wages be full from the Lord, the God of Israel, under whose wings you have come to seek refuge." Then she said, "I have found favor in your sight, my lord, for you have comforted me and indeed have spoken kindly to your maidservant, though I am not like one of your maidservants."*

> - Ruth 2:11-13 (NASB)

Look at that! Ruth went out into the field and found favor in the sight of Boaz, just as she had hoped. When she went home, Naomi was stunned at how much Ruth had come home with. When Ruth said that the man she spoke to was Boaz,

Naomi remembered that he was a close kinsman of Elimelech and tells Ruth that she should do as he says.

Boaz has hinted that he's willing to be a provider for Ruth by the way he has taken care of her so far. Ruth continues gleaning in Boaz's fields through to the end of the barley and wheat harvests.

Naomi has found her hope again, and she comes up with a bold plan to get Boaz to marry Ruth. It's bizarre and rather *risqué*. In Ruth 3:1-5, Naomi tells Ruth to put on her best clothes and look as attractive as possible. When Boaz goes to the threshing floor after celebrating the harvest, she's to follow him, uncover his feet, lie down with him and when he sees her there, to do what he tells her to do.

This plan could go off the rails quickly. Boaz could see this as an offer for sex and hie her hence, they could get caught together in the middle of the night and that would surely get tongues a-waggin' ruining both Boaz's *and* Ruth's reputation, or Boaz could give into temptation and bump uglies with Ruth. What's even weirder than this plan is that Ruth goes along with it ... sort of.

Ruth does all that Naomi tells her to do with one little exception — when Boaz wakes up and finds a dolled-up vixen curled up sleeping at his feet, Ruth doesn't give him a chance to tell her what to do, she takes the initiative and pulls a Sadie Hawkins and proposes to Boaz. She said, *"I am Ruth, your maid. So spread your covering over your maid for you are a close relative."* (Ruth 3:8) Ruth basically said, "According to God's law, you're the one who can be my husband and I'm cool with that. Let's head to Vegas, baby!"

It was a bold move and ... it worked. Boaz was even more impressed with Ruth for not trying to be noticed by a Hemsworth brother or some other younger man — she was doing things *God*'s way and His way was the kinsman redeemer.

Boaz gives her grain for Naomi and tells Ruth that there is another closer family member who could be the kinsman redeemer, but he's going to do what he can for Ruth because *"you are a woman of excellence."* (Ruth 3:11)

It all goes according to plan, and Elimelech's closer relative wasn't so keen on tying the knot with Ruth, so Boaz announces that he will do so publicly. Ruth's story ends happily and with a pretty amazing surprise — Ruth, who didn't have children with Mahlon, bears a child, Obed. The curse was clearly over.

But, because when God does things, He pulls out all the stops. Our God is a *big* God and He does things in a *big* way. (Ephesians 3:20) God didn't just bless Ruth with a son — she became the grandmother of King David, and therefore in the lineage of Jesus. (Matthew 1)

Oh, by the way, you might remember Boaz's mom from an earlier chapter — her name was Rahab. Yep, Rahab the hooker was the mother of Boaz.

Ruth was a pretty amazing woman who has shown incredible faith in the most difficult of times. She had an unwavering trust in God no matter what that brought to her in this life. She didn't think of her comfort, didn't follow God to be blessed "thirty, sixty, or a hundredfold," and she worked her tail off when she needed to. And still, she got to play a part in God's great plan to redeem mankind by being the however-many-times great-grandmother of the Messiah.

Not bad for a Moabite widow whose descendants weren't supposed to enter the assembly of the Lord for ten generations, eh?

The point is, you don't know God's plan, and sometimes, when you're at your lowest and look up, there He is ready to take you to that next level life with Him. That's what He did for Ruth.

As Paul wrote to the believers in Rome:

Who will separate us from the love of Christ? Will tribulation, or distress, or persecution, or famine, or nakedness, or peril, or sword? Just as it is written, 'For your sake we are being put to death all day long; we were considered as sheep to be slaughtered. But in all these things we overwhelmingly conquer through Him who loved us. For I am convinced that neither death, nor life, nor angels, nor principalities, nor things present, nor things to come, nor powers, nor height, nor depth, nor any other created thing, will be able to separate us from the love of God, which is in Christ Jesus our Lord.

- Romans 8:35-39 (NASB)

When God is for us, who — or what — can be against us? (Romans 8:31)

They Thought She Was Nuts, God Thought She Was Perfect

Then Hannah prayed and said,
"My heart exults in the Lord;
My horn is exalted in the Lord,
My mouth speaks boldly against my enemies,
Because I rejoice in Your salvation."

- 1 Samuel 2:1 (NASB)

Scripture says that God's timing isn't always our timing, and I don't know about you, but that's certainly been true in my life.

It looks like I'm in good company, too. Having His people wait for the right moment for His plans and purposes to come to fruition seems to be God's *modus operandi*.

Check it out:

- Abraham had to wait for Isaac.
- Jacob had to work for Laban for 14 years before he could marry Rachel.
- the Israelites wandered through the desert for *four decades* before they could enter the Promised Land.
- the Messiah came *thousands* of years after the

covenant made with Abraham.

Even now, the church is still waiting for the glorious, triumphant return of Jesus which we were assured by John the Beloved was going to happen "quickly." (Rev. 22:20)

"Quickly" clearly means something different to an eternal God than it does to those of us schleppin' this pebble, eh?

Sometimes — heck, *many* times — waiting for God to move is no fun at all.

Our culture isn't exactly known for its ability to be patient. We have instant information at our fingertips, online shopping with next-day delivery, and entertainment available to be streamed into our devices 24/7. Our modern self-centered, instant gratification, me-monkey era isn't exactly working on honing *that* virtue — or *any* virtue, really.

Scripture shows us that people in the Bible handled waiting on God in different ways:

- Abraham decided to rush the promise along by having Ishmael with Hagar, which worked out with such spectacular results that you can see the effects in the Middle East to this day.
- The Israelites whined and complained that they missed Egypt's version of "The Cheesecake Factory" while *God Himself* was before them in a cloud by day and a pillar of fire by night. They were rebellious and took the first opportunity to make an idol and worship it. God didn't take too kindly to that and their rebellion and impatience was rewarded by an extended stay in the rather rustic Camp Sand Dune.

And then, there's Hannah.

Hannah wasn't anyone special — she was a housewife.

She wasn't the 90-year old wife of the man that God had made a covenant with, she didn't hide the spies on her roof in Jericho, she wasn't called to be one of the judges of Israel, she didn't take a tent peg and hammer it through the brainpan of the leader of the Canaanite army, nor was she in the bloodline of the Kings of Israel and the Messiah that was promised.

Actually, Hannah wasn't called to any real act of greatness in her own life. She was an ordinary woman married to an ordinary man, and she wanted to live an ordinary life. Specifically, she wanted to be a mother. The problem was, like Sarai, Hannah was barren.

Hannah's husband, Elkanah, was a devout man who loved her dearly. Elkanah was *also* married to Peninnah, with whom he had several children. I'm sure you can see where this is headed, right? It's kinda like the Abraham-Sarah-Hagar or Jacob-Leah-Rachel situations — one woman has kids, but the other can't.

Here's the twist with Hannah's tale ... she didn't react the way that Rachel and Sarah did. She didn't hand over her handmaiden to bear children for her or ask that Peninnah be banished. Although, that last one might've crossed Hannah's mind because scripture tells us that Peninnah wasn't a sweet, loving "sister-wife" like on some jacked-up *Life Network* show glorifying polygamy. Nah, Peninnah was a grade-A, certified biatch — at least where Hannah was concerned. Peninnah mocked Hannah for not being able to have kids and rubbed it in that she had been blessed with many children.

This constant emotional abuse took its toll on Hannah. It was so bad that she refused to eat until Elkanah encouraged her to.

When Elkanah sacrificed, he passed helpings from the sacrificial meal around to his wife Peninnah and all her children, but he always gave an especially generous helping to Hannah because he loved her so much, and because God had not given her children. But her rival wife taunted her cruelly, rubbing it in and never letting her forget that God had not given her children. This went on year after year. Every time she went to the sanctuary of God she could expect to be taunted. Hannah was reduced to tears and had no appetite.

- 1 Samuel 1:3-7 (MSG)

The trip to the House of God became an ordeal. Year after year Hannah would have to endure the nasty jibes from Peninnah.

But check out what Hannah did — she didn't gossip and tell the other women that Peninnah was a heartless old hag, she didn't a start flame-war on Facebook, and she didn't get into a catfight with her. Hannah pulled herself together, went to the temple and took her problems to God in prayer.

Then Hannah rose after eating and drinking in Shiloh. Now Eli the priest was sitting on the seat by the doorpost of the temple of the Lord. She, greatly distressed, prayed to the Lord and wept bitterly. She made a vow

and said, "O Lord of hosts, if You will indeed look on
the affliction of Your maidservant and remember me,
and not forget Your maidservant, but will give Your
maidservant a son, then I will give him to the Lord all
the days of his life, and a razor shall never come on
his head."

– 1 Samuel 1:9-11 (NASB)

You see, despite the years of not being blessed with a child, Hannah believed that God would still give her a son. God had opened up Sarah's womb when she was well past child-bearing age and Hannah knew that God could do the same for her.

Hannah was unwilling to settle for her lot in life, and she knew that God could change her situation. She was so positive of this that she even vowed that she would give her firstborn right back to God.

Maybe Hannah was thinking of 1 Chronicles 29:14, *"Everything comes from you; all we're doing is giving back what we've been given from your generous hand."*

Or maybe she was reminded of what God says to Moses in Exodus 13:2, *"Consecrate every firstborn to me — the first one to come from the womb among the Israelites, whether person or animal, is mine."*

The vow itself was a gutsy move on Hannah's part. The last time the vow to not have a razor touch the head of a yet-to-be-conceived son was with Samson. And although he is credited with some of the most incredible deeds in scripture, he also had some — shall we say — "rough patches." She would have known that, but she made the vow anyway.

Hannah was a prayer warrior. In the passage, she was so focused on her intense prayer to God that Eli the priest thought that she was drunk. She explained to him what's going on:

> *"No, my lord, I am a woman oppressed in spirit; I have drunk neither wine nor strong drink, but I have poured out my soul before the Lord. Do not consider your maidservant as a worthless woman, for I have spoken until now out of my great concern and provocation." Then Eli answered and said, "Go in peace; and may the God of Israel grant your petition that you have asked of Him." She said, "Let your maidservant find favor in your sight." So the woman went her way and ate, and her face was no longer sad.*
>
> – 1 Samuel 1:15-18 (NASB)

God *did* grant Hannah's petition, and she had a son. She named him Samuel, and, because God had kept His word, Hannah was true to hers. Once Samuel was weaned, she brought him back to the Temple.

That had to have been a really hard thing for her to do. While some parents today have trouble as they tearfully leave Junior at college, Hannah brought her toddler to the Temple to live. She had wanted nothing more than to have a child, and now that she had Samuel, she was ready to hand him over to serve God. She'd then go back home, *without* her son, to face Peninnah and her many children again. Good Lawd, that is some kind of faith!

Hannah bringing Samuel to the Temple is like a reversal

of God's interaction with Abraham — in that situation it was God that initiated the promise of a son, God asked Abraham to sacrifice Isaac, and it was God who provided an alternative sacrifice. With Hannah, *she* had made the deal with God, *she* kept her word and brought him to the temple, and God blessed both Hannah and Samuel for it.

When the family of Elkanah arrived at Temple, Hannah prayed a powerful prayer exalting God and rejoicing in Him rather than in the son that she was given. She praises God for who He is -- His holiness, His majesty, provision for His people, and, of course, how He gives the barren woman not one child, but *children*.

Then Hannah prayed and said,
"My heart exults in the Lord;
My horn is exalted in the Lord,
My mouth speaks boldly against my enemies,
Because I rejoice in Your salvation.
"There is no one holy like the Lord,
Indeed, there is no one besides You,
Nor is there any rock like our God.
"Boast no more so very proudly,
Do not let arrogance come out of your mouth;
For the Lord is a God of knowledge,
And with Him actions are weighed.
"The bows of the mighty are shattered,
But the feeble gird on strength.
"Those who were full hire themselves out for bread,
But those who were hungry cease to hunger.
Even the barren gives birth to seven,
But she who has many children languishes.
"The Lord kills and makes alive;
He brings down to Sheol and raises up.
"The Lord makes poor and rich;
He brings low, He also exalts.
"He raises the poor from the dust,

He lifts the needy from the ash heap
To make them sit with nobles,
And inherit a seat of honor;
For the pillars of the earth are the Lord's,
And He set the world on them.
"He keeps the feet of His godly ones,
But the wicked ones are silenced in darkness;
For not by might shall a man prevail.
"Those who contend with the Lord will be shattered;
Against them He will thunder in the heavens,
The Lord will judge the ends of the earth;
And He will give strength to His king,
And will exalt the horn of His anointed."

– 1 Samuel 2:1-10 (NASB)

What's pretty amazing about this incredible prayer is not just how much it looks like it was ripped right out of the book of Psalms, it also sounds a whole lot like Mary's prayer, *The Magnificat,*

Check it out:

And Mary said:
"My soul exalts the Lord,
And my spirit has rejoiced in God my Savior.
"For He has had regard for the humble state of His bondslave;
For behold, from this time on all generations will count me blessed.
"For the Mighty One has done great things for me;
And holy is His name.
"and his mercy is upon generation after generation toward those who fear him.
He has done mighty deeds with His arm;
He has scattered those who were proud in the thoughts of their heart.
"He has brought down rulers from their thrones,
And has exalted those who were humble.

"He has filled the hungry with good things;
And sent away the rich empty-handed.
"He has given help to Israel His servant,
In remembrance of His mercy,
As He spoke to our fathers,
To Abraham and his descendants forever."

-Luke 1:46-55 (NASB)

The extraordinary prayer of an ordinary housewife was reflected in the prayer of an ordinary teen over a thousand years later. Both of these women would give birth to sons who would quite literally change the world.

At the very end of Hannah's prayer, she speaks about God giving strength to His king. Remember, this was still in the time of the judges — Israel didn't have a king yet.

It would be Hannah's son, Samuel, who would anoint Israel's first kings, Saul and David.

Samuel would grow up to be Israel's greatest Judge and a prophet of God. He was wise, faithful, and 1 Samuel 3:19,20 says,

"God was with him, and Samuel's prophetic record
was flawless. Everyone in Israel, from Dan in the
north to Beersheba in the south, recognized that Sam-
uel was the real thing — a true prophet of God."

That glimpse forward in Hannah's prayer wasn't just about exalting the future kings of Israel, like David and Solomon, it also looks forward to the King of Kings who will be exalted above all. That Word of God that was in Mary's womb when she spoke the Magnificat.

Philippians 2:9-10 says:

> *"God highly exalted Him, and bestowed on Him the name which is above every name, so that at the name of Jesus every knee will bow, of those who are in heaven and on earth and under the earth."*

As for Hannah, she would go and visit Samuel every year when Elkanah went to make the sacrifice and would bring her son a new robe. God blessed Hannah with three additional sons and two daughters.

Hannah's story may not be filled with constant adventure like Sarah's or intense action like Jael's, but it is filled with a reality that so many people can relate to. Hannah's story stands out partly because she was just such a normal person with nothing particularly special about her.

Well, maybe that's not quite right …

She was a tenacious woman of faith.

Hannah refused to accept that her situation was beyond God's ability to change. She latched onto God's promise to Abraham that his children would be like the stars in the heavens and one of those would be *her* son.

Hannah took her troubles with Peninnah to God by pouring out her heart in prayer. No backbiting, no gossip, and no retaliation. She showed incredible self-control in a difficult situation.

Finally, Hannah kept her word. David would eventually write in Psalm 15:5 that someone who dwells on God's holy hill will keep his word even when it hurts him to do so.

So, Dear Reader, how do *you* handle the rut that you're in? Do you hold tight to God's promise and refuse to let go, or do you fold like a cheap tent in a hurricane saying, "Woe is me?"

Do you take your problems to God in prayer or do you go blabbing to every Tom, Dick, and Harry you come across seeking advice when Jesus says, "Ask, seek, knock"?

What about your vows … do you keep your word even if it hurts you to do it? Integrity matters to God. Does it matter to you?

Maybe we can all learn a thing or two from this ordinary woman in 1100 B.C. whose fervent prayer was heard and honored by God and the entire nation of Israel was blessed for generations because of it.

Her Sex Appeal and Her Boldness Saved A Nation

They related Esther's words to Mordecai. Then Mordecai told them to reply to Esther, "Do not imagine that you in the king's palace can escape any more than all the Jews. For if you remain silent at this time, relief and deliverance will arise for the Jews from another place and you and your father's house will perish. And who knows whether you have not attained royalty for such a time as this?"

- Esther 4:12-14 (NASB)

Have you ever been in a high-pressure situation where everything was riding on a single do-or-die decision?

Because that was Esther's story.

Do the right thing, and she might pay with her life. Chicken out, and it could cost the lives of her entire people.

If you're looking for inspiration in high-stakes courage, then Esther is your girl.

Unlike the other Jewish ladies we've been talking about, Esther is a long way from home. We don't find her in the Jewish capital of Jerusalem, or the hill country, or even in Nazareth, or Galilee.

She's not even in Israel at all. Because when Esther comes into the picture, there *is* no nation of Israel to call home. The Jewish nation has rebelled against God one too many times, and He has sold them into the hand of foreign conquerors, who burned down their nation and shipped them off to live in parts unknown.

Jews have begun moving back to their homeland, and the Temple has been rebuilt. But it just isn't the same as the glory days.

Pretty much everyone lives under the thumb of a world-conquering emperor. His empire stretches from India to Ethiopia. (Esther 1:1)

You already know this Emperor from your history books -- Xerxes I. He's the dude taunted by Leonidas with those famous words, "Molon Labe" at the Battle of Thermopylae. He's the Emperor that attacked Greece at Marathon, and who was eventually crushed by Alexander the Great.

He's the sort of powerful figure you simply do *not* say "no" to.

When Esther comes on the scene, a crooked politician has cooked up a plot getting the king to greenlight a genocide to kill every Jew in the realm -- unless a young Jewish girl can stop him.

The stakes were high.

How did we get here, and how does an orphaned Jewish girl find herself swept up into the geopolitical politics of the world's greatest superpower?

Well, it all started with a queen who didn't do as she was told.

It was the year 483 BC. The king was throwing a party. It wasn't just *any* party.

It was the kind of party you throw when you're still new to the throne and trying to solidify your political power. Leonidas didn't know it yet, but this party planner was going to strike Greece soon, and he needed everyone to be on the same page.

Xerxes' wife, Queen Vashti, was not on the same page. He didn't like that, not one little bit.

Scripture uses the name "King Ahasuerus," but it's the same guy. Here's what happened at the party gone wrong.

In the third year of his reign he gave a banquet for all his princes and attendants, the army officers of Persia and Media, the nobles and the princes of his provinces being in his presence. And he displayed the riches of his royal glory and the splendor of his great majesty for many days, 180 days.

When these days were completed, the king gave a banquet lasting seven days for all the people who were present at the citadel in Susa, from the greatest to the least, in the court of the garden of the king's palace. ... Queen Vashti also gave a banquet for the women in the palace which belonged to King Ahasuerus.

*On the seventh day, when the heart of the king was
merry with wine, he commanded Mehuman, Biztha,
Harbona, Bigtha, Abagtha, Zethar and Carkas, the
seven eunuchs who served in the presence of King
Ahasuerus, to bring Queen Vashti before the king with
her royal crown in order to display her beauty to the
people and the princes, for she was beautiful. But
Queen Vashti refused to come at the king's command
delivered by the eunuchs. Then the king became very
angry and his wrath burned within him.*

*Then the king said to the wise men who understood the
times—for it was the custom of the king so to speak
before all who knew law and justice and were close to
him: Carshena, Shethar, Admatha, Tarshish, Meres,
Marsena and Memucan, the seven princes of Persia
and Media who had access to the king's presence and
sat in the first place in the kingdom— "According to
law, what is to be done with Queen Vashti, because
she did not obey the command of King Ahasuerus
delivered by the eunuchs?" In the presence of the
king and the princes, Memucan said, "Queen Vashti
has wronged not only the king but also all the princes
and all the peoples who are in all the provinces of
King Ahasuerus. For the queen's conduct will become
known to all the women causing them to look with
contempt on their husbands by saying, 'King Ahasuerus commanded Queen Vashti to be brought in to his
presence, but she did not come.' This day the ladies of
Persia and Media who have heard of the queen's conduct will speak in the same way to all the king's princes, and there will be plenty of contempt and anger. If it
pleases the king, let a royal edict be issued by him and
let it be written in the laws of Persia and Media so
that it cannot be repealed, that Vashti may no longer
come into the presence of King Ahasuerus, and let the
king give her royal position to another who is more
worthy than she. When the king's edict which he will
make is heard throughout all his kingdom, great as it*

is, then all women will give honor to their husbands,
great and small." This word pleased the king and the
princes, and the king did as Memucan proposed.

- Esther 1:3-21 (NASB)

Why did she refuse? Was it because she was busy with running her own banquet? Was she supposed to show up at this party with a stripper pole?

Who knows? Historians are still fighting about it.

What matters is, she defied the king, and paid a price for it. Suddenly, he's shopping for a new queen. And that's where our girl Esther shows up in the story.

In his own version of *The Bachelor*, he holds himself a Miss Persian Empire contest, and Esther is one of the winners. She joins the harem. But that's not the end of the story.

She's brought in and given the best spa treatments Persian darics could buy. She quickly becomes a staff favorite, and they give her all the insider tips she could need to win the king's, uh, heart. Or something.

Four years after the party gone wrong, the time came for Esther's big night -- an overnight visit with the king.

She used her head, did some insider trading with the top eunuch about the king's naughty preferences and showed up in that cheerleader's outfit he liked so much.

The king loved Esther more than all the women, and
she found favor and kindness with him more than all
the virgins, so that he set the royal crown on her head

and made her queen instead of Vashti. Then the king gave a great banquet, Esther's banquet, for all his princes and his servants; he also made a holiday for the provinces and gave gifts according to the king's bounty.

- Esther 2:17,18 (NASB)

Esther went from being an orphaned kid raised by her kindly uncle to the queen in the king's palace. Her uncle had asked only one favor of her--that she keep her nationality a secret, which she did.

Life's pretty good for Esther and her Cinderella story, right?

Ok, not *exactly* a Cinderella story. She's a Jewish girl matched up with a pagan king, by no less than the intervention of God himself. And it's not like this is Prince Charming, either. She may have been elevated to the status of queen, but she's still just the best young lady in some middle-aged king's harem.

Here comes the plot twist. Everything goes South when her uncle, Mordecai, gets himself a powerful enemy, Haman.

Haman got promoted by the king. The king commanded that Haman should be praised, honored, and flattered by the butt-kissing public in this government town. But Mordecai wasn't the kneeling type.

When Haman learned that Mordecai was Jewish, he dreamed of genocide. He was powerful enough to hatch a plan to make it happen. All he'd have to do is convince the king that these infuriating Jews were a liability to his kingdom.

> *Then Haman said to King Ahasuerus, "There is a certain people scattered and dispersed among the peoples in all the provinces of your kingdom; their laws are different from those of all other people and they do not observe the king's laws, so it is not in the king's interest to let them remain."*
>
> - Esther 3:8 (NASB)

The king gave it a thumbs-up and passed Haman his signet ring, letting him write and authorize the edict.

> *Letters were sent by couriers to all the king's provinces to destroy, to kill and to annihilate all the Jews, both young and old, women and children, in one day, the thirteenth day of the twelfth month, which is the month Adar, and to seize their possessions as plunder. A copy of the edict to be [i]issued as law in every province was published to all the peoples so that they should be ready for this day. The couriers went out impelled by the king's command while the decree was issued at the citadel in Susa; and while the king and Haman sat down to drink, the city of Susa was in confusion.*
>
> - Esther 3:13-15 (NASB)

Her uncle heard about the plot and got word to Esther. Now we're up to speed with where we started this chapter.

The Jewish queen faced a moment of real crisis. Speak up and risk death, or say nothing and watch her people be slaughtered?

Then Mordecai told them to reply to Esther, "Do not imagine that you in the king's palace can escape any more than all the Jews. For if you remain silent at this time, relief and deliverance will arise for the Jews from another place and you and your father's house will perish. And who knows whether you have not attained royalty for such a time as this?"

Then Esther told them to reply to Mordecai, "Go, assemble all the Jews who are found in Susa, and fast for me; do not eat or drink for three days, night or day. I and my maidens also will fast in the same way. And thus I will go in to the king, which is not according to the law; and if I perish, I perish." So Mordecai went away and did just as Esther had commanded him.

- Esther 4:13-17 (NASB)

She fasts and prays ... and then she takes action. This is where the Queen Vashti part comes into play. Disobedience to the king -- even by his queen -- is a serious offence. If she shows up to the king's court unsummoned, she could pay with her life.

Problem: she hasn't been summoned to the king's presence for 30 days, and the genocide clock on the extermination of her people is already ticking.

She took that chance and threw herself at his mercy. If he is offended, she's done for. If he shows mercy, then she lives.

She came up with a plan and got everyone she knew to pray and fast.

Did you notice that nowhere in the book of Esther does it mention God by name? But His hand shows up all over the place in it.

Mordecai foiled a plot on the king's life. Esther became queen. The king couldn't sleep and remembered Mordecai's good deed.

But the biggest example ... with her life hanging in the balance, depending on the whim of the world's most powerful king, what did Esther do?

She turned to God for support, courage, and rescue.

Just like the Apostle Paul did:

And don't forget to pray for me. Pray that I'll know what to say and have the courage to say it at the right time, telling the mystery to one and all, the Message that I, jailbird preacher that I am, am responsible for getting out.

- Ephesians 6:19,20 (MSG)

She pushed all her chips onto the table, and trusted God for the result.

And she was smart about it. She used human nature and her femininity to her advantage. She didn't just blurt out her request. She built up the suspense and interest, which made Xerxes more emotionally invested in what she had to say.

Now it came about on the third day that Esther put on her royal robes and stood in the inner court of the king's palace in front of the king's rooms, and the king was sitting on his royal throne in the throne room, opposite the entrance to the palace. When the king saw Esther the queen standing in the court, she obtained favor in his sight; and the king extended to Esther the golden scepter which was in his hand. So Esther came near and touched the top of the scepter. Then the king said to her, "What is troubling you, Queen Esther? And what is your request? Even to half of the kingdom it shall be given to you." Esther said, "If it pleases the king, may the king and Haman come this day to the banquet that I have prepared for him."

Then the king said, "Bring Haman quickly that we may do as Esther desires." So the king and Haman came to the banquet which Esther had prepared. As they drank their wine at the banquet, the king said to Esther, "What is your petition, for it shall be granted to you. And what is your request? Even to half of the kingdom it shall be done." So Esther replied, "My petition and my request is: if I have found favor in the sight of the king, and if it pleases the king to grant my petition and do what I request, may the king and Haman come to the banquet which I will prepare for them, and tomorrow I will do as the king says."

- Esther 5:1-8 (NASB)

Come to the banquet. And I'll tell you then. Ok, let me spoil you with another banquet, and I'll tell you then.

And she made sure that Haman -- the same guy who plotted the Jewish nation's destruction -- was the only other person at these two banquets.

Then, in the second banquet, the big reveal.

"There is a plot against my life, O king. It's not just against me, but against my entire people."

That plot against my life was hatched by

... *(Dramatic Pause)*

... *this* guy!

Haman just realized that a trap had snapped shut. And he was inside it.

Long story short, Esther's courage saves the Jews.

Haman and his kids get hanged on the gallows they built for Mordecai. Mordecai gets to move into Haman's palace. Esther becomes a folk hero, and everyone gets a new holiday.

What's the moral of this story? What can we learn from it today?

Well, Esther and the Jewish people were targeted by a hostile bureaucracy hellbent on their destruction. Sound familiar?

The secular government bowed to no other earthly power.

It feared no human authority.

But that didn't stop Esther.

She turned to God.

She got results.

She Thought She Was Past Her Prime, She Was Wrong. Very Wrong

---

When Elizabeth heard Mary's greeting, the baby leaped in her womb; and Elizabeth was filled with the Holy Spirit. And she cried out with a loud voice and said, "Blessed are you among women, and blessed is the fruit of your womb! And how has it happened to me, that the mother of my Lord would come to me? For behold, when the sound of your greeting reached my ears, the baby leaped in my womb for joy. And blessed is she who believed that there would be a fulfillment of what had been spoken to her by the Lord."

- Luke 1:41-45 (NASB)

Have you ever gotten the silent treatment?

Was it for a long time?

An afternoon? A week? Maybe a decade?

How about 400 years? Because that's how long the children of Israel got the cold shoulder from God in this chapter.

Was God being too brutal? To answer that, we'll have to recap how God has been trying to get Israel's attention.

Throughout the Old Testament, we see Israel repeating that same, sad, cycle. Just like so many of us do.

Desperate people cry to God for help. He helps them. Life gets better. They forget about God. They make dumb choices. God lets life get bad for them again. They become desperate.

Lather, rinse, repeat.

It happened in Egypt and the wilderness.

It happened all through the book of Judges.

It happened after God gave them a golden age under David.

It happened when they started getting kicked around by their neighbors.

It happened when God sold them into captivity in Assyria and Babylon.

It happened when God brought them home again from captivity.

And they still were not getting the message.

They *still* blew off God's warning about worshipping their neighbors' gods. They ignored God's word. Some of His prophets were even put to death.

So after making it painfully clear that they would be under the thumb of foreign rulers for a very long time (see Daniel 11) -- *God stopped talking to them completely.*

He warned Israel about that silence through the prophet

Amos:

> *"Behold, days are coming,"* declares the Lord God,
> *"When I will send a famine on the land,*
> *Not a famine for bread or a thirst for water,*
> *But rather for hearing the words of the Lord.*
>
> - Amos 8:11 (NASB)

After that, a parade of foreign rulers marched through history just like Daniel said they would. We pick up the story again when the Romans were taking their turn.

Then, when nobody saw it coming, God broke His silence ... with a splash. The Lord set up a story that brought us right back to the very beginning of His relationship with Israel.

The first words after a long silence matter. This divine silence was no different.

He singled out one devout family, long past the age of child-bearing, and told them that the kid they were bringing into the world would play a big role in closing that distance between God and His beloved. Ring any bells?

Here's how the divine silence to Israel was finally broken in Luke chapter one.

> *In the days of Herod, king of Judea, there was a priest*
> *named Zacharias, of the division of Abijah; and he*
> *had a wife from the daughters of Aaron, and her name*
> *was Elizabeth. They were both righteous in the sight*
> *of God, walking blamelessly in all the commandments*
> *and requirements of the Lord. But they had no child,*
> *because Elizabeth was barren, and they were both*
> *advanced in years.*

Now it happened that while he was performing his priestly service before God in the appointed order of his division, according to the custom of the priestly office, he was chosen by lot to enter the temple of the Lord and burn incense. And the whole multitude of the people were in prayer outside at the hour of the incense offering. And an angel of the Lord appeared to him, standing to the right of the altar of incense. Zacharias was troubled when he saw the angel, and fear [k]gripped him. But the angel said to him, "Do not be afraid, Zacharias, for your petition has been heard, and your wife Elizabeth will bear you a son, and you will give him the name John. You will have joy and gladness, and many will rejoice at his birth. For he will be great in the sight of the Lord; and he will drink no wine or liquor, and he will be filled with the Holy Spirit while yet in his mother's womb. And he will turn many of the sons of Israel back to the Lord their God. It is he who will go as a forerunner before Him in the spirit and power of Elijah, to turn the hearts of the fathers back to the children, and the disobedient to the attitude of the righteous, so as to make ready a people prepared for the Lord."

Zacharias said to the angel, "How will I know this for certain? For I am an old man and my wife is advanced in years." The angel answered and said to him, "I am Gabriel, who stands in the presence of God, and I have been sent to speak to you and to bring you this good news. And behold, you shall be silent and unable to speak until the day when these things take place, because you did not believe my words, which will be fulfilled in their proper time."

The people were waiting for Zacharias, and were wondering at his delay in the temple. But when he came out, he was unable to speak to them; and they realized that he had seen a vision in the temple; and he kept making signs to them, and remained mute.

*When the days of his priestly service were ended, he
went back home.*

*After these days Elizabeth his wife became pregnant,
and she kept herself in seclusion for five months,
saying, "This is the way the Lord has dealt with me in
the days when He looked with favor upon me, to take
away my disgrace among men."*

- Luke 1:5-25 (NASB)

In case we're a little slow on the uptake, scripture makes it really, really clear that Elizabeth is no spring chicken. She's old, and so is her husband. Old like Abraham and Sarah were old. Old like Joshua in his final address.

Even her wrinkles had wrinkles.

Get it? Got it? Good.

They were old, which wouldn't be a problem, except they were also childless.

In ancient Israel, that problem carried more weight than just not having the family you had always wanted. It came with *shame,* and a lot of it.

At the top of this chapter, we skimmed over Israel's twisted history and how their sins brought down negative sanctions from heaven, but we could take the wrong lesson from that.

Sometimes life really does club you in the face with a 2x4 because you've done dumb stuff and you deserve it. Just ask Israel about their long slog through the Old Testament.

But is that what happened to *this* couple? Were they cursed because of some terrible sin in their lives? Is that the picture we get from God's word?

Nope.

It's *muy* bad theology to believe that *all* the crud that life throws your way hits you *because you deserve it*. Before we're told that Elizabeth was barren, we're told something else. Something important.

She and her husband were both *righteous, walking blamelessly in all the commandments and requirements of the Lord.* In a country best known for getting kneecapped after turning its back on God, this is a big deal.

Imagine Elizabeth's private hell.

She was a *righteous* woman living in a harsh, moralizing world that takes her barrenness as proof of some secret sin. Even Jesus's own disciples wrestled with this issue. Remember that man born blind? No? Here's the quick and dirty King Doug Authorized paraphrase:

Hey Jesus, you see that blind guy? The bros have been debating it and we'd like you to settle it. Who did the sinning? Was it this dude or his parents? I've got 20 drachma on his parents. Jesus answered, (probably with an *oy vey* and a facepalm) that they were reading the situation bass-ackwards. This blindness wasn't the result of anyone's sin. It was there to show God's greater plan at work.

For Elizabeth and her husband, that "greater plan" meant

their baby being born long after they were too old to have kids.

Back at the temple, Zacharias had waited a very long time for his number to finally come up. His turn to serve in the temple finally came. When it did come, God showed up. He dropped a dramatic miracle that would get all the faithful Jews who heard about it talking in amazement.

An angelic visitation promised that God was giving them a special baby that would change everything. Change wasn't just coming to their life, it was coming to the whole nation of Israel.

In giving them this child, God was answering their prayers for a son. Sure, it wasn't in the way they were expecting their prayers to be answered. It was in God's own way, for His own purposes. He can change things up like that -- you know, being God, and all.

The God who *"is able to do far more abundantly beyond all that we ask or think"* has a plan for our lives that can beggar even our wildest imagination.

It's a good thing, too. Because their imagination couldn't have dreamed up a prayer big enough for what God was looking to kick down the doors of hell with.

Isn't that just like God to do something like that in our lives? He'll do it in yours too, if you'll let Him.

Where were we?

Right. God was busy throwing Liz and Zack a curveball straight out of Heaven itself. What *else* did God do with Elizabeth and Zacharias? I'm glad you asked my little kiddies.

God vindicated the honor of His daughter. He proved to a skeptical world that Elizabeth had *not* committed some terrible sin to prevent God from blessing their family with children.

You can practically hear the pain, shame, and heartbreak she has carried with her all these years fall away when she says, *"He looked with favor upon me, to take away my disgrace among men."*

I was disgraced, but now I am honored! God is good and one of His good gifts is to lift that burden of shame away.

Let's skip ahead, because we'll be digging into Mary's role in this story in a different chapter.

TL;DR version: Mary, mother of Jesus gets an angelic visit, too. The angel tells her about Jesus, and as an example to stir up her faith, points to the miracle of Elizabeth's pregnancy to prepare her for the unique miracle birth she is about to experience.

Young Mary packed her suitcase, called herself an Uber and drove off to her cousin's *casa* in the country for a couple of months. What ol' Liz had to say when she showed up on her doorstep was so epic that it found its way into the *verbum Dei.*

> *Now at this time Mary arose and went in a hurry to*
> *the hill country, to a city of Judah, and entered the*

house of Zacharias and greeted Elizabeth. When
Elizabeth heard Mary's greeting, the baby leaped in
her womb; and Elizabeth was filled with the Holy
Spirit. And she cried out with a loud voice and said,
"Blessed are you among women, and blessed is the
fruit of your womb! And how has it happened to me,
that the mother of my Lord would come to me? For
behold, when the sound of your greeting reached my
ears, the baby leaped in my womb for joy. And bless-
ed is she who believed that there would be a fulfill-
ment of what had been spoken to her by the Lord."

- Luke 1:39-45 (NASB)

Remember back in verse 15, when we were told that Liz-
zie's baby would be *filled with the Holy Spirit* even *before* he
took his first breath? It's showtime!

Why would a baby even *need* to be filled with the Spirit?
Simple -- to make verse 41 possible, and Elizabeth's inspired
answer in verse 44.

This happened something like six months into that pregnancy. The little bro wasn't even born yet, but he was filled
with God's Holy Spirit. Little baby John had a reaction that
God Himself described as *joy* in the presence of Christ.

News flash: it's never "a clump of cells" that the Holy Spirit fills and moves upon. It's a person. The Bible is pretty clear
about that.

Nobody ever looked down at their bagel and lox to see it
sit up and start prophesying. Even the weirdest example in
scripture, Balaam's donkey, was a living creature.

John was still in utero, but he was *alive*, he experienced joy, and he was filled with the Holy Spirit. Yes, you read that right, I said "he." This is the Third Person of the Trinity Himself putting His marker down that yes, that unborn babe in the womb really is a person.

Gee, does that sound like a Pro-Life message? Good. You've been paying attention.

This little baby John was moved by the Holy Spirit even *before* his mother was. And then she prophesied with those well-known words, *"Blessed are you among women, and blessed is the fruit of your womb!"*

Sound familiar? The last time we heard those words, Deborah was prophesying about Jael. The righteous babe with the mallet and tent peg. This time those words are on the lips of Elizabeth, prophesying about Mary and her unborn son.

Hate to break it to you, but whatever "blessed among women" meant when God said it about *one* of those two women, He must have meant for the other one too. Don't shoot the messenger.

That's just how the logic works.

Some elaborate meanings believers pack these words with just won't fit when you try to apply them to Jael.

One meaning, though? One meaning fits like a glove. Check out the two stories from a different angle:

- Jael, using nothing but the ordinary tools of her trade

as a wife living in a tent, was the instrument God used to defeat the enemy who had oppressed Israel.

- Mary, using nothing but the ordinary gifts of her femininity, her receptivity and her capacity to bring life into the world was the instrument God used to launch a much greater victory against a much greater enemy.

Both ladies, through very simple-seeming acts, played pivotal roles in a much grander story, and were praised for their faithfulness.

God was being glorified by using an unlikely method to bring salvation to His people. Both women, for stepping up when the time came to be a willing participant in God's plan, were honored by being called "blessed."

Not to bum you out or anything, but if God's Spirit wasn't giving Jael some fancy new religious honorific, through Deborah, then that's probably not what He's doing the other time He says it, either.

Let that thought whir around in our tin brains for a bit.

I can wait.

Did you grab your smelling salts? Are you ready to move on?

Good. Me too.

Time doesn't stand still and Elizabeth didn't stay pregnant forever. Eventually that baby popped into the world with all the chaos and messiness that new life brings with it.

This was no ordinary baby, and God put on a show to make sure the world knew it.

Elizabeth is no longer living in shame and disgrace, she's delighting in God's mercy and rejoicing with the whole clan.

Her husband has been silent for the entire pregnancy. And now, it's time to name the baby. She breaks with the family tradition of naming the kid after a relative and does what the angel had told them ... named him John.

Spoiler alert: This would *not* be the last tradition this kid would be flipping on its head.

Now the time had come for Elizabeth to give birth, and she gave birth to a son. Her neighbors and her relatives heard that the Lord had displayed His great mercy toward her; and they were rejoicing with her.

And it happened that on the eighth day they came to circumcise the child, and they were going to call him Zacharias, after his father. But his mother answered and said, "No indeed; but he shall be called John." And they said to her, "There is no one among your relatives who is called by that name." And they made signs to his father, as to what he wanted him called. And he asked for a tablet and wrote as follows, "His name is John." And they were all astonished. And at once his mouth was opened and his tongue loosed, and he began to speak in praise of God. Fear came on all those living around them; and all these matters were being talked about in all the hill country of Judea. All who heard them kept them in mind, saying, "What then will this child turn out to be?" For the hand of the Lord was certainly with him.

- Luke 1:57-65 (NASB)

Did you spot how this story is different from Abraham and Sarah?

The first time around, Sarah was skeptical but Abraham believed. This time around, we see that reversed. *Zacharias* was the skeptical one, and *Elizabeth* believed.

If anyone tries to tell you that dudes are "more spiritual" or better believers than the ladies, show them this. Sometimes the bros have it together, sometimes their wives do.

Men and women lean on each other.

Elizabeth was the one who obeyed the angel's instructions in naming the kid John. Then, the God who just broke His own silence, made sure they got the message by ending Zacharias's silence at the same time.

> *And his father Zacharias was filled with the Holy Spirit, and prophesied, saying:*
> *"Blessed be the Lord God of Israel,*
> *For He has visited us and accomplished redemption for His people,*
> *And has raised up a horn of salvation for us*
> *In the house of David His servant—*
> *As He spoke by the mouth of His holy prophets from of old—*
> *Salvation from our enemies,*
> *And from the hand of all who hate us;*
> *To show mercy toward our fathers,*
> *And to remember His holy covenant,*
> *The oath which He swore to Abraham our father,*
> *To grant us that we, being rescued from the hand of our enemies,*
> *Might serve Him without fear,*
> *In holiness and righteousness before Him all our days.*
> *"And you, child, will be called the prophet of the Most*

High;
For you will go on before the Lord to prepare His ways;
To give to His people the knowledge of salvation
By the forgiveness of their sins,
Because of the tender mercy of our God,
With which the Sunrise from on high will visit us,
To shine upon those who sit in darkness and the shadow
of death,
To guide our feet into the way of peace."
And the child continued to grow and to become strong
in spirit, and he lived in the deserts until the day of his
public appearance to Israel.

- Luke 1:67-80 (NASB)

Elizabeth may have only had the one child in her old age. But what a child that was!

Her legacy, whether she lived long enough to see it play out or not, was amazing. She brought a child into the world that tore a ragged scar in Satan's backside.

He was the Prophet of the Most High, who turned the hearts or the fathers back to the children and children back to their fathers. That voice crying in the wilderness, *"Make straight the paths of the Lord."*

Jesus Himself weighed in on the significance of the son she had brought into the world at a hinge point of history:

"Truly I say to you, among those born of women there has not arisen anyone greater than John the Baptist!" – Matthew 11:11 (NASB)

Elisabeth's heart's desire was a very simple and ordinary one -- she wanted a family. She got that, and a whole lot more.

If You're A Teenage Girl from A Crap Town, Get Ready for A God Thing

Now in the sixth month the angel Gabriel was sent from God to a city in Galilee called Nazareth, to a virgin engaged to a man whose name was Joseph, of the descendants of David; and the virgin's name was Mary. And coming in, he said to her, "Greetings, favored one! The Lord is with you." But she was very perplexed at this statement, and kept pondering what kind of salutation this was. The angel said to her, "Do not be afraid, Mary; for you have found favor with God. And behold, you will conceive in your womb and bear a son, and you shall name Him Jesus. He will be great and will be called the Son of the Most High; and the Lord God will give Him the throne of His father David; and He will reign over the house of Jacob forever, and His kingdom will have no end."

- Luke 1:26-33 (NASB)

M ary.

You know, Jesus' mother. What did she actually *look* like?

If you had to help a police sketch artist come up with a

picture of her, what would the sketch look like?

Would she be a lady in her 20s or 30s, standing tall with a serene and regal bearing, wearing some brightly colored blue or red clothes? Maybe she's on the back of a donkey and heavy with child? Maybe she's surrounded by straw in a stable?

Or would you sketch out a regular peasant girl, wearing rough, plain-colored clothes? Draw her as a kid in what, maybe the ninth grade?

Is that picture shocking to you? Good. Because shaking things up was kind of the *point* of Christ dropping in on this planet, wasn't it?

He could have seen to it that He was born into a regal household -- He was descended from a line of kings, after all. He wasn't brought up wearing Brooks Brothers or walking the royal gardens. He came to grow up in a frontier town on the back-half of nowhere, but He made a point of being born into a very ordinary life. Mary, a very ordinary peasant girl, was part of that plan.

Hold up, did we just call Mary ordinary?

Yep. In a lot of ways, she was. That's *exactly* what makes the miracle of her divine Son so special.

Jesus, fully God, had a birth that flipped the ordinary way of producing a child on it's head. A mom that had never knocked boots with anyone? Yep. That'll do it. This way, He was clearly something *more* than just another human.

But He was also *fully* human. What does that mean? He had to share the life experiences of the rest of us. More than that, if He was going to save us from our sins, He had to come *from* one of us -- from Mary.

Jesus was sinless. That's the easy part believers can all agree on. Here comes the part that gets dicey for some folks. Buckle up.

The question is asked, "how could a sinful person produce a sinless child?" Struggling with that answer, the religious "experts" come up with an explanation: maybe God did a miracle in Mary so that she was sinless from the moment she was conceived, so that she could be worthy of being Jesus' mother? That's a very popular theory in some circles.

Does that popular theory hold up? Well, Dinky, let's open The Book and have a look.

How does she start her famous inspired song, *The Magnificat?*

> *"My soul exalts the Lord, And my spirit has rejoiced in God my Savior."*
>
> - Matthew 1:46-47 (NASB)

"God *my Savior,*" she tells us.

Ok, class, very good. And what *is it* that God saves us from? That's right, sin. That's a gold star for you.

Mary is acknowledging that -- just like the rest of us -- she is mortal and fallible. This makes the story of faithfulness in that scared little girl all the more powerful.

Don't think for a minute she didn't know what the risks were. One way or another, the bottom was about to drop out of her serene little world.

She knew what would happen if Joseph assumed the worst about her. Which he did, until an angel talked him out of breaking off the wedding.

She knew how Jewish culture treated *that* sort of a woman -- let alone when it was a girl her age! She knew the hit her reputation would take -- and how people would talk. She surely felt all of those feelings.

But there was something about Mary. She saw something more.

Mary saw that a God who had stood silent for 400 years was already up to something new. She saw that her wrinkly relative Elizabeth was six months pregnant and married to a man who had been struck dumb since the moment he saw the angelic vision concerning the child God had given her.

Change is in the air. It was electric. She found herself living in a time of miracles. Not just "out there" somewhere, either. God's miraculous hand had already been at work -- in her own family. Gabriel explicitly reminded her of that fact ...

The angel answered and said to her, "The Holy Spirit will come upon you, and the power of the Most High will overshadow you; and for that reason the holy Child shall be called the Son of God. And behold, even your relative Elizabeth has also conceived a son in her old age; and she who was called barren is now in her sixth month. For nothing will be impossible with God." And Mary said, "Behold, the bondslave of the Lord; may it be done to me according to your word." And the angel departed from her.

- Luke 1:35-38 (NASB)

"Nothing will be impossible with God," she was reminded.

What God could do despite the limitations of Elizabeth's age, He could also do despite the limitations of Mary's youth. And that spark fanned her faith into flame.

This God really *is* the God of the impossible.

"Ok, then," she said. "I'm in."

And just like that, she stepped into history. She met God on the same terms as all the other great, yet imperfect, people of scripture had. She met Him by faith, by trusting and obeying.

That faith *is* the miracle. She believed *despite* the limitations of her youth and frail human nature. We don't need to explain it away with another special miracle that Scripture never mentions.

What else is amazing about Mary? She was a great example for believers to copy in a number of ways. We'll get to that. But we've got another sacred cow or two to drop onto the BBQ first.

If we're going to honor her properly, we have to do it by the book -- the *verbum Dei*. If even *angels* had to tell the apostles not to kneel to anyone but God, we need to make sure we're not out of line in how we show our own respect, either.

> *I, John, am the one who heard and saw these things.*
> *And when I heard and saw, I fell down to worship at*
> *the feet of the angel who showed me these things. But*
> *he *said to me, "Do not do that. I am a fellow servant*
> *of yours and of your brethren the prophets and of*
> *those who heed the words of this book. Worship God."*
>
> - Revelation 22:8,9 (NASB)

The gospels have several places where they could teach us about how to properly respect Mary. But the way Jesus Himself uses those teachable moments makes the typical uber-religious take on Mary *verboten*.

Don't take my word for it. Let's go Berean and crack open that Book again.

There Jesus is, dropping truth-bombs in the public square, confounding the Pharisees and showing compassion to the ordinary Joe (or maybe Jacob?) when an enthusiastic fangirl comes up to cheer Him on, with a very typical Middle Eastern twist on praising Him:

> *While Jesus was saying these things, one of the*
> *women in the crowd raised her voice and said to Him,*
> *"Blessed is the womb that bore You and the breasts at*

which You nursed."

– Luke 11:27 (NASB)

They were offering indirect praise to Jesus, and direct praise to Mary herself. That should be cool with Him, right? But it wasn't. It continues:

But He said, "On the contrary, blessed are those who hear the word of God and observe it." – Luke 11:28 (NASB)

Ouch. Shot down.

The fangirl was missing the point and Jesus said so. The focus of what He came here for is *not* about praising Mary, it's about connecting directly to God in a life marked by repentance and transformation.

But surely the Mother of God is owed some kind of special place of honor, isn't she? Let's go back to the Book:

While He was still speaking to the crowds, behold, His mother and brothers were standing outside, seeking to speak to Him. Someone said to Him, "Behold, Your mother and Your brothers are standing outside seeking to speak to You." But Jesus answered the one who was telling Him and said, "Who is My mother and who are My brothers?" And stretching out His hand toward His disciples, He said, "Behold My mother and My brothers! For whoever does the will of My Father who is in heaven, he is My brother and sister and mother."

- Matthew 12:46,50 (NASB)

It was an ordinary conversation. While Jesus was going about His Father's business, proclaiming a message of hope and repentance to the crowd, someone got a message to Him ... "Hey Jesus, Your family is here. And they want a word with You."

You can only imagine what they might want to talk to Him about. Maybe to ask Him if He was ever coming back to work at Joseph & Sons Carpentry Co. Maybe to ask Him if He was in over His head with His new public speaking gig. His own brothers hadn't even figured out what was going on yet. We know this because the Gospel of John told us so:

> *"His brothers said, "Why don't you leave here and go up to the Feast so your disciples can get a good look at the works you do? No one who intends to be public-ly known does everything behind the scenes. If you're serious about what you are doing, come out in the open and show the world." His brothers were pushing him like this because they didn't believe in him either."*
>
> *- John 7:3-5 (MSG)*

Jesus used the reference to His own family as a teaching opportunity.

"... is my brother and sister and mother."

Notice Jesus chose His words carefully. He did not say "Father." There's a good reason He didn't do so. That role -- obviously -- is taken by One alone. The Father in the Triune Godhead.

If the role of His mother was to be seen as uniquely special and significant as some keep telling us, this would be the perfect place to say so. Jesus could have exempted "mother" from His example in the same way he exempted "father." Why didn't He just say "brother and sister?" That would have been clean, simple, and would have left room for an elevated view of Mary.

Exactly. Why *didn't* He? We'll let you chew on that for a minute. Read it again slowly. Use a lifeline if you have to. Maybe phone a friend.

Gawrsh. I'm just a public school kid, but even my whirring tin brain can figure out that if He said it that way He probably meant it that way. Maybe so that we wouldn't miss the point and put her on a pedestal?

On that topic of brothers and sisters, you all know exactly what the next sacred cow headed for the grill is going to be, right? You guessed it. The virginity question.

The Bible is clear about Mary having "never been with a man" at the time of the miraculous conception. She was a virgin when Jesus was born. That *is* the miracle. Done and dusted, no question, no contest. Her maidenly purity is uncontested

The next part is more controversial. Nowhere does it say that she should be reasonably expected, as a properly married woman, to spend the rest of her days in a cold marriage bed. Nor does it say that Joseph should be condemned to that either.

The Bible talks about other kids in the family. And even if you tapdance around how they might not have been *her* kids, the townsfolk (who insulted Jesus by implying He was a bastard) sure thought they were:

> *"Where did this man get these things, and what is this wisdom given to Him, and such miracles as these performed by His hands? Is not this the carpenter, the son of Mary, and brother of James and Joses and Judas and Simon? Are not His sisters here with us?" And they took offense at Him.*
>
> - Mark 6:2,3 (NASB)

Here's the problem with saying Mary was a perpetual virgin -- it creates the same sin problem it tries to solve.

People trying to defend Mary's honor portrayed her as a "perpetual virgin" in an effort to elevate her and make her somehow more morally pure. But doing that actually creates the opposite problem.

For one thing, married sex isn't dirty or sinful at all. Only the *illicit* kind of sex is.

> *Marriage is to be held in honor among all, and the marriage bed is to be undefiled; for fornicators and adulterers God will judge.*
>
> - Hebrews 13:4 (MSG)

If you think God is anti-sex, you should read the Song of Solomon sometime. If you understand what you're reading, it's steamy enough to make any teenage boy blush. And it's ... *scripture*! In fact, marriage and sanctified sex is the *remedy* for sin in people whose libidos run a little too hot.

> *But if they do not have self-control, let them marry;*
> *for it is better to marry than to burn with passion.*

> - 1 Corinthians 7:9 (NASB)

What does the Bible say about a sexless marriage? Simple: it is not God's plan. Notice the language of *mutual* moral obligation to the sexual needs of the other spouse.

> *The husband must fulfill his duty to his wife, and*
> *likewise also the wife to her husband. The wife does*
> *not have authority over her own body, but the husband*
> *does; and likewise also the husband does not have*
> *authority over his own body, but the wife does. Stop*
> *depriving one another, except by agreement for a time,*
> *so that you may devote yourselves to prayer, and come*
> *together again so that Satan will not tempt you be-*
> *cause of your lack of self-control.*

> - 1 Corinthians 7:3-5 (NASB)

So, if Mary's marriage bed was cold, it doesn't make her some kind of a super-saint. It just trades the supposedly awkward "moral problem" of her having done the deed with a different moral problem -- unlawfully withholding herself from her lawful husband.

We'll let those sacred cows cook on the grill for a while and go back to the ways she is an example to the believer.

Mary wasn't the kind of person to rush to judgment. Again and again she was struck by something amazing about the life of her Son and she "pondered these things in her heart." She let all these things percolate inside and shape her thinking.

The shepherds shared their story. Mary treasured it, pondering it in her heart. When Jesus was twelve, left behind in the city and spent 3 days blowing the minds of the Big Dawgs in the Temple, when Jesus said He must be in His Father's house? She tucked that away into her heart.

Decades later, all of those ponderings played a role in Jesus's very *first* miracle.

At the wedding feast in Cana, there was a crisis. The wine for the guests was running out. This was a Big Deal, capital B, capital D, for first-century Jewish families, and such an event would be a source of great public shame.

Somebody in the know came to Mary about the problem. Mary didn't have a solution. But she knew Someone who might. After all, this is the guy who, at 12 years old, was running circles around the religious experts.

"Whatever He says to do, do it."

She wasn't expecting a miracle, necessarily. Jesus, in His time schlepping this pebble, had never before performed one. No, not even that clay birds story some people love to tell. John 2:11 contradicts any claims of an earlier miracle.

Mary was just expecting Him *to be Jesus,* the guy you turn to when you need help with something. She probably figured

He had a great insight that could help them solve this problem.

She had confidence in Him. All she said was "Whatever He says to you, do it."

Others saw her confidence in Him and trusted Him also. That sentence set the stage for the first miracle in the Gospels.

Inspiring others to believe in Jesus is a big deal. *The* big deal, even.

She didn't go to Jesus on their behalf. She sent them to the Source Himself. Her role was done. The baton was passed. It was her Son's turn to shine.

What was true then is true now. She knew about Jesus and His willingness to help directly. She didn't *intercede* for the wedding guests, she pointed the way to see the solution for themselves.

There is one verse in scripture that echoes this same idea.

1 Timothy 2:5 says:

For there is one God, and one mediator also between God and men, the man Christ Jesus, who gave Himself as a ransom for all, the testimony given at the proper time.

The Message says it this way:

He wants not only us but everyone saved, you know, everyone to get to know the truth we've learned: that there's one God and only one, and one Priest-Media-

tor between God and us—Jesus, who offered himself in exchange for everyone held captive by sin, to set them all free.

It doesn't matter how you say it, Jesus Himself is the *only* direct connection to the Father. We don't need to send someone else on our behalf. Jesus *was* that Someone Else on our behalf.

But what if we screw it all up? We were going to. Period.

Jesus already knew it. He saw it coming a mile away. But it changes nothing. He will bridge that gap anyway. His love for us is enough that we don't need to send any messenger He loves more to intercede on your behalf.

That's the key point. It isn't that we overestimate Mary's worth. It's that we underestimate His love for us. Jesus Himself ever lives to intercede for us. (Hebrews 7:25)

Yes, even His love for little ol' you.

But what about that moment during His crucifixion, when Jesus told John "behold your mother." If all this other stuff is true, what's that all about?

Jesus was the eldest son in His family. It was His job to make sure that His widowed mother had food, shelter, and was well cared for.

Even in that moment of weakness and pain, He kept the commandment to *"Honor thy mother and thy father."* Jesus wouldn't be around to look after that. Obviously.

Jesus passed that burden of responsibility to someone He could trust. He was asking John to fulfill that role of "son" in her life, since He could no longer do so Himself.

Mary was a wide-eyed kid from a no-horse town who believed God was still a God of miracles. When He spoke, she listened. When she saw people with a problem that only Jesus could solve, she pointed them to Him.

She's more like us than you think.

And one heck of an example to follow.

She Went from Being Demonized, To Being One of Jesus' Favorite Ladies

---

*Jesus said to her, "Woman, why are you weeping?
Whom are you seeking?" Supposing Him to be the
gardener, she said to Him, "Sir, if you have carried
Him away, tell me where you have laid Him, and I
will take Him away." Jesus said to her, "Mary!" She
turned and said to Him in Hebrew, "Rabboni!" (which
means, Teacher). Jesus said to her, "Stop clinging
to Me, for I have not yet ascended to the Father; but
go to My brethren and say to them, 'I ascend to My
Father and your Father, and My God and your God.'"
Mary Magdalene came, announcing to the disciples,
"I have seen the Lord," and that He had said these
things to her.*

- John 20.15-18 (NASB)

I've said before in this tasty little tome that God picks
the unlikeliest people to be a part of His fellowship. Yes,
my dear little Christian, He sometimes selects people who
many would just dismiss. And that's very good news indeed!
It means there's hope for all of us.

This time, I'm not talking about the sin-laden crowd who were adulterers, liars, and murderers, but the awkward ones. God's Hall of Fame is filled with people that a lot of Christians might find themselves uncomfortable with -- Gideon was timid, Moses stuttered, and Samson was rebellious. What could these three have in common besides being children of Abraham? Well, they're all listed in Hebrews 11 as examples of people who showed what it means to walk by faith. It looked very different for each of them, but they're all still listed there.

We've got a very motley crew in the New Testament, too. Just check out The Twelve — you've got some rough-hewn, cussin' fishermen, a tax collector, a doubter, a guy who wasn't so keen on people from Nazareth (now there's some irony!), a political revolutionary, a traitor, and a couple of former Baptists — as in followers of John the Baptist. These men (aside from Judas Iscariot, of course,) shook the whole known world for Christ and most of them were killed for it. But they weren't alone in their devotion to Jesus. As a matter of fact, most of the 11 abandoned Jesus when the fit hit the shan at His arrest and trial — only John didn't run for the hills. Another of Jesus' most faithful followers was there, too, a woman named Mary.

Women were an important part of Jesus' ministry. He didn't treat them as less than men — they were allowed to sit at His feet and listen to His teaching. This view of equality was something unusual at the time. Women noticed. Although Jesus had many faithful female followers, the one most mentioned in the New Testament is Mary.

Mary Magdalene is mentioned just a dozen times in scripture, but we can still get a pretty good picture of this awesome woman of God.

When Jesus was on His Book Tour, He was out there saying crazy things like *"love your enemy"* and *"let he who is without sin, cast the first stone."* The religious leaders thought He was nuts.

Then, He was healing people and casting out demons and they were *positive* that He was nuts. His followers were probably off their rockers, too. That might have been because some of those same people that had been healed and had devils cast out of them became faithful followers of Jesus.

Mary Magdalene had seven demons cast out of her.

Hold up a sec … was that *seven demons?*

Indeed. Scripture says it was even demons.

Doesn't that seem like a great candidate for a small group leader?

Now, I don't know about you, but before I met God, I was an absolute mess. Still, as jacked-up as my life was pre-Christ, I don't think it was *infested with seven demons* messed-up. If that's *your* story, well, then bully for you, Dinky! You can relate to Mary Magdalene on a level that some of us non-demon-possessed folk can't.

The very first mention of Mary's name in the Gospel of Luke includes the tidbit that she had an exorcism.

Soon afterwards, He began going around from one city and village to another, proclaiming and preaching the kingdom of God. The twelve were with Him, and also some women who had been healed of evil spirits and sicknesses: Mary who was called Magdalene, from whom seven demons had gone out, and Joanna the wife of Chuza, Herod's steward, and Susanna, and many others who were contributing to their support out of their private means.

– Luke 8:1-3 (NASB)

In just three verses we learn quite a bit about Mary:

- She was from Magdala, a fishing town on the Sea of Galilee.
- She was tormented by seven demons until Jesus put the kibosh on that.
- She wasn't mentioned in connection to another person as the wife, daughter, or sister.
- She contributed to the ministry out of her private funds.

Yes, kiddies, Magdalene isn't her last name, it's a reference to the town where she came from — just like Jesus of Nazareth or Simon of Cyrene. It's a helpful little note to differentiate her from the many other women named Mary, and more concise than reminding everyone that she had been the host to seven demons prior to meeting Christ. Although, the Gospels do mention that a few times.

Scripture notes that Mary was a giver. She was providing for the ministry of Jesus. Can you just imagine a convo between a couple of the Apostles?

John: "Mary just donated some more money for the ministry."

Peter: "Oh? Do you mean the sister of Lazarus?"

John: "Nope. The other Mary — the one that had seven demons cast out of her."

Peter: "Ah. The one from Magdala. Gotcha."

The seven demons thing was a *really* big deal. There was social ostracism and stigma to those who suffered from the torment of demons. Back in those days, being a vessel for a legion of hellish fiends was frowned upon. Now it'll probably get you a record deal and a Grammy.

Remember that time in John chapter 9 that Jesus and the Twelve came across a man who was blind from birth and Jesus healed him by making mud with His spit and wiping it on the dude's eyes? The Apostles asked Him what had caused the blindness — the man's sin or his parents? (FYI: That wouldn't have been *my* first question, after watching the Son of God slap spit-mud in some dude's eyes.)

Now imagine the questions about a woman tormented by *seven demons.* What kind of things could she possibly have been involved in to have that many devils take up residence? Imagine what that speculation was like. Maybe she was worshipping idols, listening to "demon music" or into some kinky sex stuff.

It must have been a horrendous thing that Mary had to endure. If anyone could claim to be socially awkward it was probably the lady tormented by demons. It's not exactly something that would get her invited to parties.

No wonder she became so faithful a follower of Christ. Imagine the freedom that she had been given by having those devils sent out of her!

The Bible doesn't mention any other relation to Mary Magdalene, so it's unclear if she was married. Some church leaders think that she was betrothed to John the Evangelist, but that isn't clearly stated in scripture. Whatever her situation was -- either married or single -- she still had money that she was willing to donate to Jesus' ministry.

There's actually been quite a lot of speculation about exactly who Mary Magdalene was and some pretty wild theories about what she was to Jesus, but we're not going to get into that here. We're just digging into what *scripture* says about Mary, not pop culture, crappy movies, Broadway musicals, or church tradition — especially the weird teachings from a certain Pope round about 590 A.D. You can look those up another time ... or not. You're probably better off sticking to scripture rather than speculation.

The one thing that Mary Magdalene is known for *isn't* that she had seven demons cast out of her, but that she was there as Jesus hung on the cross and she was the first person to see Him after His resurrection.

*But standing by the cross of Jesus were His mother,
and His mother's sister, Mary the wife of Clopas, and
Mary Magdalene. When Jesus then saw His mother,
and the disciple whom He loved standing nearby, He
said to His mother, "Woman, behold, your son!" Then
He said to the disciple, "Behold, your mother!" From
that hour the disciple took her into his own household.*

*After this, Jesus, knowing that all things had already
been accomplished, to fulfill the Scripture, said, "I am
thirsty." A jar full of sour wine was standing there; so
they put a sponge full of the sour wine upon a branch
of hyssop and brought it up to His mouth. Therefore
when Jesus had received the sour wine, He said, "It
is finished!" And He bowed His head and gave up His
spirit.*

- John 19:26-30 (NASB)

Mary and several other women were present when most
of the disciples had hightailed it out of there and left Jesus
to save their own skins. She stood and watched as the Son
of God who had saved her from the torment of demons was
now being put to death in an excruciating way. She stood at
the cross as He breathed His last breath. She was there when
Joseph of Arimathea took Jesus' body down from the cross
and followed to see where His body was being taken.

*Joseph of Arimathea came, a prominent member of the
Council, who himself was waiting for the kingdom of
God; and he gathered up courage and went in before
Pilate, and asked for the body of Jesus. Pilate won-
dered if He was dead by this time, and summoning the
centurion, he questioned him as to whether He was already dead. And ascertaining this from the centurion,*

he granted the body to Joseph. Joseph bought a linen cloth, took Him down, wrapped Him in the linen cloth and laid Him in a tomb which had been hewn out in the rock; and he rolled a stone against the entrance of the tomb. Mary Magdalene and Mary the mother of Joses were looking on to see where He was laid.

– Mark 15:43-47 (NASB)

Mary had faithfully followed Christ in His life and ministry -- now she was going to make sure that He was honored in His death. She made a mental note of where His body was taken so that she and the other Mary could return and properly prepare the body for burial after the Sabbath.

There was a problem, though … who was going to roll away the stone in front of the tomb? It would have been a huge problem if it hadn't already been done. Jesus had risen from the dead. Mary and the other Mary were acting in faith not knowing that little detail — they were determined to give Jesus a proper burial.

When the Sabbath was over, Mary Magdalene, and Mary the mother of James, and Salome, bought spices, so that they might come and anoint Him. Very early on the first day of the week, they came to the tomb when the sun had risen. They were saying to one another, "Who will roll away the stone for us from the entrance of the tomb?" Looking up, they saw that the stone had been rolled away, although it was extremely large. Entering the tomb, they saw a young man sitting at the right, wearing a white robe; and they were amazed. And he said to them, "Do not be amazed; you are looking for Jesus the Nazarene, who has been cruci-

fied. He has risen; He is not here; behold, here is the place where they laid Him. But go, tell His disciples and Peter, 'He is going ahead of you to Galilee; there you will see Him, just as He told you.'" They went out and fled from the tomb, for trembling and aston- ishment had gripped them; and they said nothing to anyone, for they were afraid.

- Mark 16:1-8 (NASB)

But that was only the beginning … so much more was about to happen.

Check it out how John describes it:

Early in the morning on the first day of the week, while it was still dark, Mary Magdalene came to the tomb and saw that the stone was moved away from the entrance. She ran at once to Simon Peter and the oth- er disciple, the one Jesus loved, breathlessly panting, "They took the Master from the tomb. We don't know where they've put him."

Peter and the other disciple left immediately for the tomb. They ran, neck and neck. The other disciple got to the tomb first, outrunning Peter. Stooping to look in, he saw the pieces of linen cloth lying there, but he didn't go in. Simon Peter arrived after him, entered the tomb, observed the linen cloths lying there, and the kerchief used to cover his head not lying with the linen cloths but separate, neatly folded by itself. Then the other disciple, the one who had gotten there first, went into the tomb, took one look at the evidence, and believed. No one yet knew from the Scripture that he had to rise from the dead. The disciples then went back home.

But Mary stood outside the tomb weeping. As she

wept, she knelt to look into the tomb and saw two angels sitting there, dressed in white, one at the head, the other at the foot of where Jesus' body had been laid. They said to her, "Woman, why do you weep?"

"They took my Master," she said, "and I don't know where they put him." After she said this, she turned away and saw Jesus standing there. But she didn't recognize him.

Jesus spoke to her, "Woman, why do you weep? Who are you looking for?"

She, thinking that he was the gardener, said, "Mister, if you took him, tell me where you put him so I can care for him."

Jesus said, "Mary."

Turning to face him, she said in Hebrew, "Rabboni!" meaning "Teacher!"

Jesus said, "Don't cling to me, for I have not yet ascended to the Father. Go to my brothers and tell them, 'I ascend to my Father and your Father, my God and your God.'"

Mary Magdalene went, telling the news to the disciples: "I saw the Master!" And she told them everything he said to her.

- John 20:1-18 (MSG)

It wasn't one of the Twelve that Jesus first spoke to after the resurrection — it was the *señorita* that had seven demons knocked out of her. The woman that faithfully sat at His feet, supported His ministry out of her own pocket, and stayed as He hung on the cross. The woman who brought spices to embalm His body after He was unjustly executed.

It seems rather fitting, no?

Jesus also tells her that He is going to ascend to His Father. He flips the same idea spoken by Ruth to Naomi telling Mary to tell the disciples, "Where *I* will go, *you* will go. Your people *are* My people, and *My* Father is now *your* Father."

And yet, after all of that faithful devotion — being there for the crucifixion when the disciples went into hiding, standing at the cross as Jesus died, following where His body was going to be laid, and then being the first person that saw Him after His resurrection, check out how Mark describes the events:

> *Now after He had risen early on the first day of the week, He first appeared to Mary Magdalene, from whom He had cast out seven demons. She went and reported to those who had been with Him, while they were mourning and weeping. When they heard that He was alive and had been seen by her, they refused to believe it.*
>
> -Mark 16:9-11 (NASB)

She's still called the woman who had seven demons cast out of her.

Thanks, Mark.

But, actually … thanks, Mark! This brings up an important point — there are some people that will only ever fixate on your past, not the transformation that happens when you truly meet Jesus. They'll only ever see Mary as the woman who had seven demons tormenting her, and they'll only see you in the light of your mistakes. Did that stop Mary from her tireless devotion to Jesus in life and even after His death? Nope. She kept on going.

Mary Magdalene showed a faithfulness and devotion that flowed from a changed heart and a transformed life.

Just like so many of the other women we've looked at, she was an ordinary woman.

Her story is different, though.

She didn't *do* great things in her ordinary womanliness — she was a witness to the greatest of *all* things — the resurrection.

It seems fitting that this book ends with a woman who is badass not for what *she* has done, or the way that God has used her, but as a woman who had her life changed by Jesus and her reaction to that was steadfast, unwavering devotion — even at the darkest hour.

Maybe you were tormented by seven demons like Mary was, and maybe you weren't, but it doesn't really matter. We all struggle with sin, people who see us in the light of our past, and our own self-doubt. But Mary had her head set right and had the right perspective — she kept her eyes fixed on Jesus.

Do you see what this means — all these pioneers who blazed the way, all these veterans cheering us on? It means we'd better get on with it. Strip down, start running — and never quit! No extra spiritual fat, no

parasitic sins. Keep your eyes on Jesus, who both be-
gan and finished this race we're in. Study how he did
it. Because he never lost sight of where he was headed
— that exhilarating finish in and with God — he could
put up with anything along the way: Cross, shame,
whatever. And now he's there, in the place of honor,
right alongside God. When you find yourselves flag-
ging in your faith, go over that story again, item by
item, that long litany of hostility he plowed through.
That will shoot adrenaline into your souls!

- Hebrews 12:1-3 (MSG)

So, Dear Reader, are you going to let the weirdness of your past, the opinions of others, or the roadblocks in life — like a big, ol' stone covering a tomb — get in the way of your devotion? Or will you persevere to the end?

One Last Observation

Well, that's it, ladies.

If these ten epic *señoritas'* stories, that you just plowed through, did not light a Holy Ghost fire under your backside and stoke your faith to embrace the "impossible" then your wood is wet.

As a dude, these ladies and their holy feats, both encouraged me and rebuked me for being an unbelieving and sometimes craven little evangelical dipstick worm.

What also struck me about these sisters was the diversity within this crew.

They weren't clones. Nowadays, churches spit out clones. These chicks were more varied than the voices inside of Pelosi's head.

They didn't have the same calling.

One's assignment was not "better" or "more important" than the others.

The age gaps, between the girls God commissioned, were huge. Ergo, there's no "perfect age" there's just a perfect God who uses imperfect peeps.

Also, from a purity standpoint, the Lord of All the Earth worked with and through everything from a virgin to a whore and He still does. Don't let anyone tell you otherwise.

In addition, most of these ladies would probably not be chosen by the religious hoity-toities of our day, but God chose them.

All the aforementioned should give you hope.

God uses overlooked people. He doesn't care what your age is, how much you've sinned, what your weaknesses are, or yada yada yada.

The thing He cares about is, will you believe Him when He calls you to do stuff that'll curl your hair. That's it. He can fix all the other crap. He just wants a scrappy lady who says, "giddy up" when God calls her name.

One thing's for certain: as much as the lassies differed from one another they were definitely similar in the exhibition of this one primal trait: they were bold. Yep, when God got a hold of them, they exhibited godly boldness in the face of daunting situations. And guess what, girls? So will you. Now, go and get busy. And remember, always stay rowdy.

About The Author.

Doug earned his Bachelor of Fine Arts degree from Texas Tech University and his certificates in both Theological and Biblical Studies from Knox Theological Seminary (Dr. D. James Kennedy, Chancellor). Giles was fortunate to have Dr. R.C. Sproul as an instructor for many classes.

Doug Giles is the host of ClashRadio.com, the co-founder and co-host of the Warriors & Wildmen podcast (660K downloads) and the man behind ClashDaily.com. In addition to driving ClashDaily.com (260M+ page views), Giles is the author of several #1 Amazon bestsellers including his most recent book, If Masculinity Is "Toxic", Call Jesus Radioactive.

Doug is also an artist and a filmmaker and his online gallery can be seen at DougGiles.Art. His first film, Biblical Badasses: A Raw Look at Christianity and Art, is available via Amazon Prime Video.

Doug's writings have appeared on several other print and online news sources, including Townhall.com, The Washington Times, The Daily Caller, Fox Nation, Human Events, USA Today, The Wall Street Journal, The Washington Examiner, American Hunter Magazine, and ABC News.

Giles and his wife Margaret have two daughters, Hannah and Regis. Hannah devastated ACORN with her 2009 nation-shaking undercover videos and she currently stars in the explosive, 2018 Tribeca Documentary, Acorn and The Firestorm.

Regis has been featured in Elle, American Hunter, and Variety magazines. Regis is also the author of a powerful new book titled, How Not to Be A #Me-Too Victim, But A #WarriorChick.

Regis and Hannah are both black belts in Gracie/Valente Jiu-Jitsu.

Speaking Engagements

To invite Doug to speak at your next event, log on to Doug-Giles.org and fill out the invitation request.

Accolades for Giles include …

– Giles was recognized as one of "The 50 Best Conservative Columnists Of 2015"

– Giles was recognized as one of "The 50 Best Conservative Columnists Of 2014"

– Giles was recognized as one of "The 50 Best Conservative Columnists Of 2013"

– ClashDaily.com was recognized as one of "The 100 Most Popular Conservative Websites For 2013 and 2020"

– Doug was noted as "Hot Conservative New Media Superman" By Politichicks

Between 2002 – 2006, Doug's 3-minute daily commentary in Miami received seven Silver Microphone Awards and two Communicator Awards.

What others say about Doug Giles

For a generation, at least, Western Society has been leveling its ideological guns on men -- that is on males, "maleness". For a good chunk of that stretch, Doug Giles -- author, hunter, commentator, broadcaster -- has taken up the cause of his fellow "dudes". His latest salvo in this desperately needed pro-XY chromosome crusade is If Masculinity Is 'Toxic', Call Jesus Radioactive. Delivered in the lively, inimitable style those familiar with Doug have come to recognize, the book confronts modern-day misandry, head on. The significance of dads, husbands, sons, brothers -- men! -- has become one of the gasping and endangered themes of our effeminized, gender-addled era. With the release of this newest tome, Doug aims to pump some life back into that foundational truth. If Masculinity Is 'Toxic', Call Jesus Radioactive tracks through the Gospel of Matthew -- a winning, easy-to-follow format -- highlighting how Jesus demonstrates what God expects of men. For all that, the book goes a long way toward sketching much of what the Creator envisions for every person -- so the ladies will benefit from perusing these pages as well.

Steve Pauwels
Editor-In-Chief, DailySurge.com

"Giles aims his arrows at the pusillanimous pastors who have bred a generation of mamby pamby Christian men who cower before the wicked. Giles challenges 'Rise up O men of God!'"

- Steven Hotze, MD
Hotze Health & Wellness Center

Doug's podcast can be seen and heard at

ClashRadio.com.

Books by Doug Giles

If Masculinity is 'Toxic' Call Jesus Radioactive

Would Jesus Vote For Trump?

Rules For Radical Christians: 10 Biblical Disciplines for Influential Believers

Pussification: The Effeminization Of The American Male

Raising Righteous And Rowdy Girls

Raising Boys Feminists Will Hate

Rise, Kill and Eat: A Theology of Hunting From Genesis to Revelation.

If You're Going Through Hell, Keep Going

My Grandpa is a Patriotic Badass

A Coloring Book for College Cry Babies

Sandy Hook Massacre: When Seconds Count, Police Are Minutes Away

The Bulldog Attitude: Get It or ... Get Left Behind

A Time To Clash

10 Habits of Decidedly Defective People: The Successful Loser's Guide to Life

Political Twerps, Cultural Jerks, Church Quirks

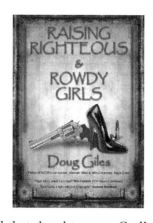

It has been said that daughters are God's revenge on fathers for the kind of men they were when they were young. Some would say that both Doug Giles and I, given our infamous pasts, are charter members of that club. However, Doug and I know that his two wonderful daughters and my equally wonderful daughter and two granddaughters are truly God's fantastic gift. With the wisdom of hindsight and experience Doug has written the ultimate manual for dads on raising righteous and rowdy daughters who will go out into the world well prepared- morally, physically, intellectually and with joyful hearts- to be indomitable and mighty lionesses in our cultural jungle. Through every raucous and no-holds-barred page, Doug, the incomparable Dad Drill Sergeant, puts mere men through the paces to join the ranks of the few, the proud, and the successful fathers of super daughters. The proof of Doug Giles' gold-plated credentials are Hannah and Regis Giles- two of the most fantastic, great hearted and accomplished young ladies I have ever known. This is THE BOOK that I will be giving the father of my two precious five and three year old granddaughters. Tiger Mom meet Lion Dad!

— Pat Caddell

Former Fox News Contributor —

Made in the USA
Coppell, TX
09 January 2024

27494655R00098